FILEY

FROM FISHING VILLAGE
TO EDWARDIAN RESORT

MICHAEL FEARON

BLACKTHORN PRESS

Blackthorn Press, Blackthorn House
Middleton Rd, Pickering YO18 8AL
United Kingdom

www.blackthornpress.com

ISBN 978 1 906259 06 8

© Michael Fearon 2008

All rights reserved. No part of this publication may be reproduced, stored in a retrieval system or transmitted, in any form or by any means, electronic, mechanical, photocopying, recording, or otherwise, without the prior permission of the Blackthorn Press.

ILLUSTRATION CREDITS

The publisher and author are grateful to the following for help with providing illustrations: Filey Museum, Anthony Avery.

Maps and Illustrations

The *front cover* shows an early impression of Filey Spa which was situated on Carr Naze. As a result of erosion, nothing now remains. John Bell's drawing was printed by Theakston of Scarborough.

1. Filey, now in North Yorkshire	*page 1*
2. The Rock Strata are very evident in this view of Filey Brigg	*page 2*
3. The 'Roman Jetty' or The Spittals which extends south-easterly from the Brigg	*page 6*
4. St Oswald's Church	*page 10*
5. John Paul Jones's ship the *Bonhomme Richard* is pictured in battle with the British ship *Serapis* on September 23, 1779	*page 24*
6. Filey in Pre-enclosure Days	*page 26*
7. A busy day in the Bay in Filey's very early days as a holiday resort.	*Page 30*
8. Built in 1857 the Filey Methodist Day School served the community until 1908. The building is now Dixon's T.V. Store.	*Page 32*
9. Clearly seen in this 1880s view of the sea-front are two boat-building yards and the primitive sea defences.	*Page 34*
10. A valued study of the craftsmen who built the Ebenezer Methodist Chapel; it opened in June 1871.	*Page 36*
11. The Filey section of the East Yorkshire Artillery Volunteers about 1898.	*Page 37*
12. A print published by Rock and Co in January 1872.	*Page 39*
13. In the 1880s a boat builder's premises stood on the present day Deepdene site.	*Page 40*
14. Queen Street about 1900.	*Page 43*
15. For a hundred years the Crescent Hotel was one of Britain's leading hotels.	*Page 45*
16. The informal church parade after Sunday morning service about 1905.	*Page 49*
17. The South Crescent Gardens about 1905.	*Page 50*
18. An earlier bandstand in the North Crescent Garden about 1910.	*Page 52*
19. Unfortunately, the identity of this Edwardian days Crescent Gardens band is not known.	*Page 53*
20. The Nansen Café stood on the Brigg where the Ornithological Group now has its hide.	*Page 54*
21. A tree-lined Station Avenue as seen in Edwardian days.	*Page 55*
22. Motor trials, 12th June 1905.	*Page 60*
23. Thomas Marr was one of several Filey butchers.	*Page 64*
24. The Royal Filey Pierrots on the beach about 1920.	*Page 65*

25. This race meeting took place on the 15th September 1923; the 1½ mile race was for the Filey Tradesmen's Cup. *Page 66*
26. Shortly before World War II, holiday-makers enjoy a day on the beach. *Page 67*
27. The Ravine Hall in use as an hotel in the 1930s. The Glen Gardens Café now stands there. *Page 69*
28. For many on holiday in the 1930s (and later) it was essential to hire a beach tent. *Page 70*
29. Cargate Hill and Kingston Cottage about 1930. *Page 72*
30. The Crescent Gardens in the mid-1950s. *Page 77*
31. Martin's barrier was built by Edwin Martin to protect his Ravine Hall estate. It was severely damaged in the storm of January, 1953. *Page 78*
32. Built in 1904, Deepdene was a family home on the sea-front until the 1960s. *Page 79*
33. Belle Vue Street and the Royal Hotel, about 1885. *Page 83*
34. Fishermen's cottages in Queen Street; to the regret of many, they were demolished in the mid 1960s. *Page 84*
35. Queen Street today. *Page 85*
36. John Wilkes Unett's plan for New Filey in 1835. *Page 86*
37. Mr and Mrs James Robinson stand outside their Beach Cottage in September 1905. *Page 89*
38. The Priest's door at St Oswald's Church. *Page 97*
39. The nave of St Oswald's Church. *Page 99*
40. Harvest Festival at the Ebenezer Chapel about 1920. *Page 105*
41. A late Victorian view of the Railway Station. *Page 108*
42. End-of-term for pupils at Mr. J. H. Daniel's private school, South Crescent. The school later transferred to Southcliffe, Primrose Valley. *Page 111*
43. Gathering news from George 'Bunny' Scales, Billy Robinson and George 'Baltic' Boynton is Lister Reekie, Editor of 'The Filey News'. *Page 115*
44. Filey Gardens in 1880. *Page 126*
45. An aerial view of Butlin's Holiday Camp from the overhead cable system. *Page 137*
46. The outdoor pool at Butlin's. *Page 138*
47. Yawls were designed to sit securely on the sand; the crew of *Tranquillity*, skipper William Ross, clean the hull, about 1890. *Page 143*
48. This post-card was entitled 'Filey Fishwife'. Unfortunately, her name is not given. *Page 144*
49. Until the 1980s fish was auctioned on the Coble Landing. *Page 146*
50. Mending nets at the top of Church Hill. *Page 147*

51. Retired fishermen meet at the end of Queen Street. *Page 148*
52. Gathering shell-fish for bait from Filey Brigg and the rocks towards Scarborough was mainly the work of Filey's young and not so young women. *Page 149*
53. Bringing boats ashore with horses was always been a skilful operation; this particular recovery took place in the 1950s. *Page 152*
54. Cork life-jackets were clearly not comfortable to wear. *Page 154*
55. Veteran Filey fisherman Healand Sayers is the raconteur in this photograph reminiscent perhaps of the celebrated picture 'The Boyhood of Raleigh'. *Page 156*
56. A Filey Yawl in Scarborough Harbour with Mark Scotter (skipper), Matthew Wright, William Cammish, George Cammish, John William Jenkinson and Reuben Scotter. *Page 158*
57. Cobles on shore and yawls in the Bay create a busy scene about 1900. *Page 159*
58. Lifeboat Day about 1905; the Filey Band waits to follow the lifeboat into Mitford Street as pierrots collect from onlookers. *Page 163*
59. Modern Filey. *Page 173*
60. Filey Beach in 2008. *Page 176*

A NOTE ON WEIGHTS, MEASURES AND MONEY

The weights, measures and monetary values used in this book are the ones contemporaries used. These may be summarised as:

Money:
4 farthings	=	1d (penny)
12d (pence)	=	1s (shilling)
1s	=	5p
20s (shillings)	=	£1 (pound)
21s (shillings)	=	1 guinea

Weight:
16oz (ounces)	=	1lb (pound)
1lb	=	0.45 kilograms
14lb (pounds)	=	1 stone
1 stone	=	6.35 kilograms
2 stones	=	1qr (quarter)
1qr	=	12.70 kilograms
4qr (quarters)	=	1cwt (hundredweight)
1cwt	=	50.80 kilograms
20cwt	=	1 ton
1 ton	=	1.02 tonnes

Volume:
2 pints	=	1 quart
1 quart	=	1.14 litres
4 quarts	=	1 gallon
1 gallon	=	4.55 litres
2 gallons	=	1 peck
1 peck	=	9.09 litres
4 pecks	=	1 bushel
1 bushel	=	36.40 litres
8 bushels	=	1qr (quarter)
1 quarter	=	2.91 hectolitres

Distance:
12in (inches)	=	1ft (foot)
1ft	=	0.305 metres
3ft (feet)	=	1yd (yard)
1yd	=	0.91 metres
22yds (yards)	=	1 chain
1 chain	=	20.12 metres
10 chains	=	1 furlong
1 furlong	=	201.17 metres
8 furlongs	=	1 mile
1 mile	=	1.61 kilometres

Area:
30¼ sq yds	=	1 perch
1 perch	=	25.29 sq metres

40 perches = 1 rood = 1210 sq yds = 1011.56 sq metres
4 roods = 1 acre = 4840 sq yds = 0.405 hectares

Prepared by Stephen Harrison

CONTENTS

		Page
Introduction		*viii*
Preface:	**The Geological Story**	1
Chapter I:	**From Earliest Times To The Norman Conquest**	4
	Pre History; Roman; Fifth -Tenth Centuries; Norman Conquest and Domesday Book	
Chapter II:	**Medieval Village To Enclosed Township**	14
	Late Medieval; Landed Families; Sixteenth Century; Seventeenth Century; Eighteenth Century; John Paul Jones; Enclosure	
Chapter III:	**The Victorians Build A New Town**	29
	Nineteenth Century; Victorian Filey; A Slightly Tarnished Image; The Promenade	
Chapter IV:	**Peace and War**	48
	Twentieth Century; Edwardian Filey; Early Flying Days; The Motor Car Comes To Filey; World War I; Between The Wars; World War II; Post-War Filey	
Chapter V:	**The Town**	82
	Buildings; Old Filey; The Churches; The Railway; Education; The Press; Elections; People	
Chapter VI:	**The Resort**	121
	The Resort; The Spa; The Crescent Gardens; Visitors; The Royal Connection; Pierrots; Butlin's	
Chapter VII:	**The Sea**	142
	Fishing; The Lifeboat; Shipping; Smuggling; Filey Harbour	
Chapter VIII	**Recent Developments**	172
Appendix A:	Population Statistics	178
Appendix B:	Some Filey Name Variations	179
Sources of Information		180
Index		183

INTRODUCTION

In several respects Filey is an ideal town about which to write a history. Its size is such that it has in its development a sufficient number of interesting aspects to provide material for a story of reasonable length; however, it is small enough to retain a real sense of community for its residents, and to engender in its many visitors a genuine feeling of affection; both these functions make easier the task of retailing Filey's story through the years.

In its growth Filey has the two strands of land and sea; for many centuries it was a village settlement resembling in several ways hundreds of others across England, but its involvement with the sea, and in particular fishing, has contributed many additional elements of enterprise, courage and drama. The development of the town as a holiday resort over one and a half centuries is in itself a story of Victorian vision and zeal, and Filey's niche in early aviation history is certainly worth more than a passing reference.

Of necessity much has been omitted; for instance the long story of Filey and fishing is worthy of a much more detailed study, which one hopes it may some day receive.

As a community Filey continues to change and no doubt this process will go on. It is surely to be wished that the courage, resourcefulness and sense of community so often displayed in past years will feature no less in Filey in the future.

THE GEOLOGICAL STORY

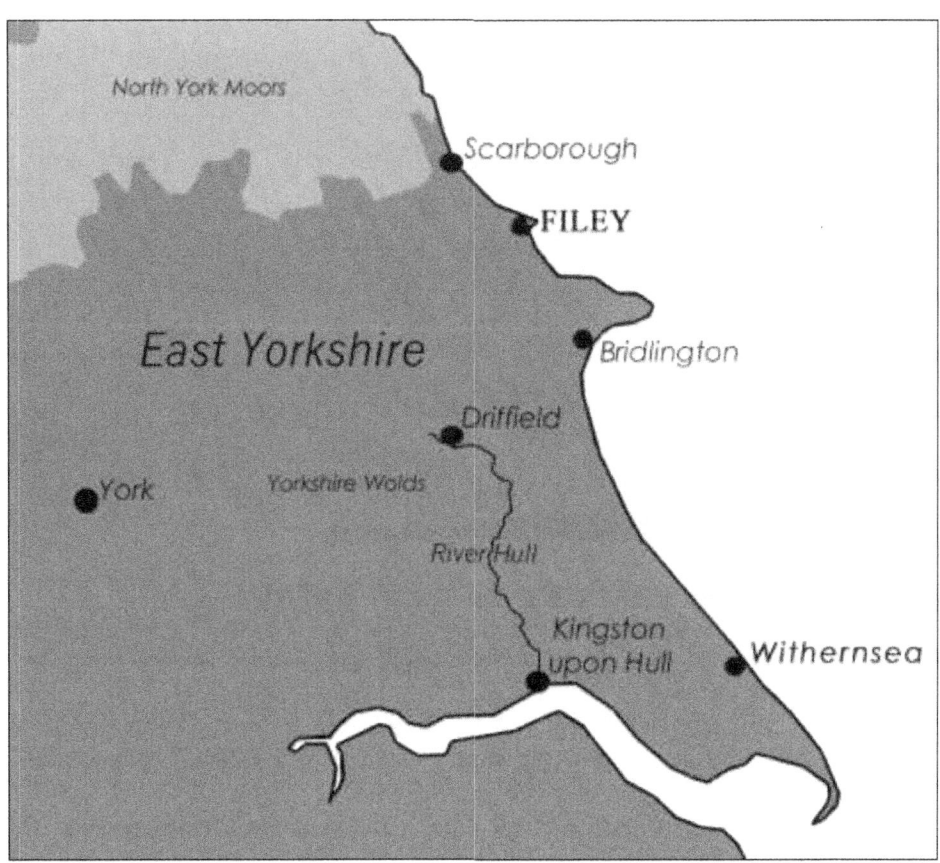

1. Filey, now in North Yorkshire.

The manner in which a community becomes established and subsequently develops depends very much on its locality. The fertility of the surrounding land and the reliability of fresh water springs are, of course, two of the major factors which were considered by the founders of many early communities. In the case of Filey the surrounding area consisted mainly of a fairly heavy clay soil which was reasonably productive. The clay was deposited during the most recent glaciation which is believed to have ended about 15,000 years ago. Glacial movement of ice over rock scrapes particles from it which are carried along by

2. The Rock Strata are very evident in this view of Filey Brigg.

the ice to be left when the ice melts. Carr Naze and the cliffs around Filey Bay were formed in this way.

Satisfying that other basic need, very reliable springs in Church Ravine supplied excellent water, though at some cost in terms of labour to those who carried it home to Queen Street.

For those interested in much older geological history, Filey Bay has much to offer. In fact, few other similarly sized areas in the United Kingdom have as great a variety of geological features for examination. Looking northwards, immediately to be seen on the side of Carr Naze is a series of sharp ridges and steep gullies where the till (alternatively known as boulder clay or glacial deposit) has weathered into badland relief — an unusual type of formation. The clay of Carr Naze rests, however, on rock which may be almost 10,000 times as old. The rock of the Brigg is mainly that which is described as Middle Calcareous Grit and was laid down as a sea-bed over a period of millions of years by marine deposition. This process continues today as river-borne material is carried to the sea. Its age is estimated to be about 150 million years. Because of the inclination of the rock which slopes downward at about 10° from north to south, the lowest exposed layers on the north side of the Brigg are rather older and are classified as Lower Calcareous Grit. Both types are of the Upper Jurassic period and contain many fossils.

Filey Bay has been formed by erosion of the soft boulder clay between the hard rock of the Brigg and the hard chalk of Bempton Cliffs and Flamborough Head. The Bay is only a few miles wide but the difference between the formations of the aforementioned materials is great. Chalk was formed as a result of the accumulation on the sea-bed of the remains of tiny marine creatures known as foraminifera and of microscopic algae. This process took place in warm, shallow waters into which little river-borne material was carried. The chalk is several hundred feet thick, indicating that deposition took place over a very long period of time.

The Upper Chalk of Flamborough Head is estimated to have an age of about 70 million years, the Middle Chalk of Thornwick Bay about 85 million years and the Red Chalk first seen in the vicinity of Speeton Cliffs about 100 million years.

The chalk, first seen clearly in Filey Bay, extends southward beyond the Wash though sometimes covered by boulder clay as in Holderness; a borehole at Hornsea revealed 40 m of clay above 260 m of chalk. A revealing aspect of time is obtained by reflection that the average rate of deposition was about 1 mm thickness of chalk every 200 years.

There are also clays in the vicinity of Reighton Gap which are very much older than the boulder clays which sometimes obscure them as erosion causes cliff slippage. There is first the black shaley Kimmeridge Clay which is Jurassic and about 135 million years old, and then the blue Speeton Clay which is a little younger. The Speeton Clay particularly has been a good source of fossils.

An unexpected occurrence is the presence of a small group of rocks on the beach opposite Primrose Valley. However, they are only revealed at intervals of several years at exceptionally low tides and low sand levels.

There is still much to be learned about Filey Bay, and local geological research continues to add to the understanding of our immediate environment; also new techniques increase our knowledge of the ways in which our familiar landscape came into being.

CHAPTER ONE

From Earliest Times to the Norman Conquest

Pre-History

Geologists estimate that as recently as 15,000 years ago, this part of the country was covered by ice. As the climate became milder the ice slowly melted and, perhaps for the first time, humans were seen here some 12,000 years ago. They survived by hunting, fishing and gathering what ever grew wild and was palatable. Their mode of life would no doubt be nomadic and dependent upon the seasons. They, or their ancestors, would almost certainly have arrived from the continent without the necessity of crossing water, as at that time there was a land-bridge where is now the English Channel.

That period is sometimes described as Mesolithic (Middle Stone), so called because tools were made of stone, and the people were of the type known as Maglemosian, a forest culture named after a pre-historic site in Denmark. Some of these folk would certainly be familiar with the region close to Filey since one of the most important of their sites was excavated in the late 1940s by Professor J.G.D. Clark at Star Carr near Flixton. The location is marked on some older O.S. maps at reference 027810. Nothing is now to be seen there, but the Rotunda Museum in Scarborough has an excellent display relating to the excavation. The dwelling places revealed had been erected about nine thousand years ago by the side of the lake which occupied much of the Vale of Pickering and the low ground between Seamer and Muston.

At about the same period in history as the occupation of the Star Carr site, a most important stage in human development was taking place in the Middle East. This was the gradual adoption by a people, previously nomadic, of a more settled way of life as a result of their new found ability to grow cereals to provide themselves and their stock with a major food source. It was, however, several thousand years before this new way of life reached these islands.

The introduction of farming here may also have had to wait for a people who could build sea-worthy vessels since the land-bridge joining England and the continent was breached in about 5000 B.C.

Later groups of people were of the Neolithic (New Stone) period which extended from about 3000 B.C. to 1800 B.C. Their burial mounds have been found on the Wolds and were of the long barrow type. Neolithic peoples found the light, dry soils of the Wolds suitable for their primitive farming methods.

Later movements of peoples with more developed skills introduced, about 1800 B.C., the Bronze Age to Britain. Again, burial mounds of Bronze Age people have provided archaeologists with much information. The mounds were of the Round Barrow type and several have been found in the vicinity of Filey; Willy Howe near Wold Newton is one. The tallest standing stone in Britain, that at Rudston, is also of the Bronze Age.

About 500 B.C. people yet more skilled in the use of metal, the Celts, began to arrive in Britain and so the Iron Age began here. Many found the Wold area suitable for their way of life especially as the climate was then rather warmer than it is now. They developed a form of horse-drawn wheeled vehicle, an example of which was found in the claypit near Hunmanby railway station. The largest cemetery in Britain so far discovered of this period occupied much of the ground between Burton Fleming and Rudston. There are indications that the particular tribe who settled in this area came from the region around Paris and thus were known as *Parisi*.

Iron Age people were occupying England when Julius Caesar came on two brief campaigns in 55 and 54 B.C. Almost 100 years later Claudius crossed the Channel and the conquest of Britain began, and with it the era we know as Roman.

There are few pre-historic archaeological sites in, or close to Filey. However, the O.S. 6" map of 1854 marks Eller Howe on the golf course at 118794 and names the beach at Martin's Ravine as Eller Howe Haven. Several stone axes, flint scrapers and arrow heads have been found. A stone axe head was found in a Muston Road garden in 1964.

One of the most remarkable discoveries in the vicinity took place in July 1834 when a tumulus on Gristhorpe Cliff was opened to reveal a 7 foot long oak log hollowed out and containing the skeleton of a 6 foot tall man. Of the Bronze Age, he was clearly a man of importance who lived about 3500 years ago and is known, not surprisingly, as the Gristhorpe Man. He resides now in the Rotunda at Scarborough. Of about the same period are the two very rare carved chalk cylinders found in a tumulus on Folkton Wold. They are now in the British Museum.

Roman Filey

Roman soldiers were probably seen in the vicinity of what is now known as Filey Bay about A.D. 70.

Julius Caesar undertook brief expeditions to Britain in 55 and 54 B.C. but not until 43 A.D. did the Romans return, this time under Claudius. It was, however, several years before the Roman Army was sufficiently in control of southern and central Britain to be able to cross the Humber and establish garrisons at Malton and York.

3. The 'Roman Jetty' or The Spittals which extends south-easterly from the Brigg.

There is some archaeological evidence that a Roman road existed from Malton to the coast at Filey, and on occasions, when road or building works have been carried out in or near Scarborough Road, foundations have been revealed which appeared to be associated with a Roman road.

The Romans were competent seamen and it is reasonable to assume that they were familiar with Filey Bay. There is however, nothing to substantiate legends associating the *Emperor's Bath,* a large rock pool on the Brigg, with the Emperor Constantine! Another local tradition, that deep ruts in the rock of the Brigg were cut by the Romans dragging their boats out of the water, is just as fanciful.

But what of the *Roman Jetty?* This is something which has intrigued and perplexed many over a long period of time. In 1828 Cole described it as 'The Spittal Rocks which are conjectured to have formed, at some very remote period, either a pier, or a foundation for one'. In order to see clearly this 'pier' it is necessary to be in the vicinity of the Brigg (Carr Naze is an excellent vantage point) at low tide during those times of the year when *spring* tides occur. These happen when Sun and Moon pull together rather than against each other and produce higher high tides and lower low tides than usual. Tide tables which can be bought locally indicate these times.

In construction the pier is about 180m long and 7m wide and extends from the Brigg in a south-easterly direction. The line of the pier is quite distinct from that of the Brigg and it joins it close to the extreme reach of Carr Naze, pointing towards Bempton Cliffs. Composed of rocks and boulders, it is sea-weed covered and its upper surface varies little from the horizontal. When exposed by the sea it provides the explorer with a scramble which is slippery but not particularly difficult.

That it is known by some as the *Roman* Jetty or Pier is not in itself significant. An object known to be old but of uncertain origin was sometimes given such a description. For instance, Danes Dyke near Flamborough and Danes Graves north of Driffield are of earlier ages than their titles suggest.

The puzzle concerning the Spittals is whether or not it is man-made. It could be thought that there would be little doubt about the construction of something so large. Those who believe it is of natural construction describe it as a cranch; that is an accumulation of boulders resulting from tidal action. This was the opinion formed by a group, including Mr. Gerald Simpson of the Yorkshire Roman Antiquities Committee and Mr. Thomas Sheppard (Curator of Hull Museum), which surveyed the formation in March 1922. Others, however, doubt very much that the tides could have achieved such an effect.

An underwater survey was carried out by 60 diving members of the Yorkshire Federation of Sub-Aqua Clubs on 4th June 1972. They made several searches in calm water with visibility of about 4 feet, but were not able to form definite conclusions about its origin.

Many consider that because of the regularity of its features, its construction could not have occurred naturally. If this is so, the problem concerning who built it remains. It is hardly likely to be pre-Roman; the Anglo-Saxons and Norsemen seldom used stone as a building material and if it was of later construction there would surely be some written record.

The Romans, however, were undaunted by the challenge of building on a large scale in stone, as indicated by Hadrian's Wall. So, perhaps it was the Romans who constructed it!

The Roman Signal Station

If there is uncertainty and controversy about the origins of the *Roman Pier* there is general agreement about the only substantial group of Roman remains found in the vicinity of Filey. By the late 4th century A.D., the Romans had been in Britain for over three hundred years and many generations of Britons had lived out their lives under Roman rule. Although there were long periods of stability during these centuries there were also times when attacks from the north by Picts, from Ireland by the Scots and by the Saxons from N.W. Europe led to many battles.

Internal dissension between Roman Army commanders and attacks by the Goths on Rome itself resulted in troops being withdrawn from Britain at a time when they were much needed for defence.

In Eastern Yorkshire, Malton was a Roman garrison town of great importance and the base from which troops could be rapidly deployed to those parts of the coast where trouble from Saxon raiders was expected. As part of the early warning system, signal stations were erected at intervals along the coast which were able to signal to each other and inland to Malton. Stations have been discovered along the Yorkshire coast at Filey, Scarborough, Ravenscar, Goldsborough and Huntcliff. Almost certainly there would be others in Holderness, but if so, presumably because of coastal erosion, none has been discovered.

It was as a result of a fall of cliff on Carr Naze in October 1857, close to its narrowest section, that it became apparent that there was something there of archaeological interest. The Rev. Richard Brooke, the then owner of Carr Naze, arranged for an examination of the site to take place and this revealed walls of large stones with tooled surfaces set in mortar. The walled area was rectangular and about 60 feet long by 25 feet wide. Within the walls were five large stones arranged as the corners of a square of side about 17 feet with one stone at the centre. It is generally accepted that these stones formed the bases for pillars on which rested a superstructure which supported a beacon. In addition to the stones there were also found two quernstones, about 40 coins and a considerable quantity of pottery. Bones of farm animals were found on the site in profusion and also many small items of wear and domestic use. An upper quernstone was discovered on the site in the 1930s.

The indications were that the structure had been severely damaged and then set on fire which suggests that it had been overwhelmed by raiders, presumably from the sea. The base stones can now be seen in the Crescent Gardens.

There have been other occasional Roman finds in the Filey area and O.S. Map Sheet TA17 (1957) indicates that pottery was found at Primrose Valley in 1924. It is likely that due to cliff erosion other Roman artefacts have long ago been lost to the sea.

The Romans knew York as Eboracum and Malton as Derventio; it is interesting to speculate what name they gave to the signal station here; another detail we shall never know.

It is estimated that 410 A.D. was about the time when soldiers of the Imperial Army were last seen in Britain. The local inhabitants must have viewed with trepidation the reduction in strength of those on whom they had relied for defence, particularly if they had observed on the horizon the square sails of Saxon raiders. However, the day they feared finally came and more than three centuries of Roman rule in Britain were over.

Fifth – Tenth Centuries

After the Romans left, there lay ahead for this part of the land a long period of instability with the area around Filey seeing the arrival of many invaders from across the North Sea. Contemporary records from the centuries following the Romans' departure are very rare and their scarcity is one reason why this period is sometimes known as the Dark Ages.

The invaders who took advantage of the inability of the native Britons effectively to defend their land, are usually known as Angles and Saxons. They came respectively from what is now Denmark and Northern Germany, and many of their number were skilled seamen with sea-worthy vessels capable of carrying immigrant families. It is likely that Filey Bay with its firm beach was a favoured entry point for these new arrivals.

One of the means by which their pattern of settlement can be traced is by looking at hamlet, village and town names. Almost no Celtic or British names survive, which suggests that it was by no means a peaceable transition period. Though real evidence is slight it seems most probable that some of the earlier inhabitants would retreat westwards, some would lose their lives in battle, and others would be absorbed willingly or otherwise into the life and culture of the Anglo-Saxons. A question unanswered, and one that most probably will remain so, is whether there was a civilian settlement here in Roman times. Perhaps there was one close to the coast; if there was, any remains will have been lost to coastal erosion.

The origins of the name of Filey are not precisely known. It may have Anglo-Saxon roots of *fif* and *leah* meaning *five clearings* or it could be derived from the Norse word, *fifa* for cotton-grass. It would be surprising if the Anglo-Saxon period passed without there being a settlement here so perhaps the first alternative is the more likely, especially when bearing in mind the remarkable sequence of Anglo-Saxon *tun* (meaning settlement) villages from Muston westwards as far as Malton.

Unlike the Romans, who were skilled in building in stone, the Anglo-Saxons seldom used stone and relied very much on wood. Consequently almost nothing that was built above ground remains of that period. The 1980s excavations close to the A64 known as the Heslerton Parish Project have revealed an Anglo-Saxon settlement which apparently lasted for about 200 years from the 5th to 7th centuries. The occupiers of this site apparently achieved quite a high standard of living in substantial timber dwellings and their way of life would no doubt be typical of many such settlements in the district, though nothing similar has been found very near to Filey.

An intriguing relic of a later period remains. In St. Oswald's tower spiral stair, a carved stone has been built in as a step. The inscribed pattern is a type of plait similar to that which is also seen embellishing the Lindisfarne Gospels. It is thought likely to have been originally a cross shaft or a grave slab similar to

4. St Oswald's Church.

those at St. Gregory's Minster, Kirkdale. The eighth century has been suggested as its period of carving and if correct this would mean that it pre-dates St. Oswald's by about 400 years. Does the presence of this stone imply that Filey had a church centuries before the present parish church?

The greater part of the movement of Anglo-Saxon peoples across the North Sea probably took place during the 6th and 7th centuries so that by the 8th century relatively settled conditions were maintained with Filey being part of the Kingdom of Northumbria which stretched from the Humber to the Forth. However, by the late 8th century a pattern of invasion similar to that of three centuries earlier was to occur. Viking raiders from the fjords of Norway began to appear on the coast with plunder as their aim. The relative ease with which they were able to rob coastal communities and monasteries encouraged others to make the voyage across the North Sea. In later years it was the Danes, whose ancestors had moved to lands vacated by the Angles, who settled in the area between the Humber and the Tees. This region became part of what was known as the *Danelaw;* the term applied to the part of England which was administered by Scandinavians.

In the 10th century most of England was unified under English Kings with the Danes and English overcoming some of their differences. Later Viking invasions affected Southern rather than Northern England and as the watershed of Hastings approached, Filey was still part of the Earldom of Northumbria now ruled by Morcar.

The Norman Conquest and Domesday Book

The years prior to and following the Norman Conquest in 1066 were some of the most dramatic and significant in the whole of English history.

In early 1066 King Edward, called *Confessor,* died without there being a clear line of succession. Harold's claim to the throne was by no means universally approved but was sufficiently strong for him to gain the crown.

In the early autumn, Harald Hardrada, King of Norway, having assembled a considerable force, sailed to the Shetlands and Orkneys then down the coast, and, according to the Orkney Saga, landed at Scarborough where the invaders destroyed much of the town by fire.

Following another landing in Holderness, the fleet sailed on up the Humber Estuary and River Ouse to take and occupy York. Soon after, the Norwegians were defeated by Harold at the hard-fought battle of Stamford Bridge.

It is not difficult to imagine the fear and anxiety that must have gripped any inhabitants of Filey who witnessed, perhaps from Carr Naze, the sacking of Scarborough by Harald and then saw the fleet sail south past the Brigg. They must have felt considerable relief as the long ships continued on course for Flamborough Head.

Harold's exultation at his victory at Stamford Bridge was soon cut short by news that William had landed on the south coast. Though exhausted by one battle, the English army hastened south to another momentous engagement near Hastings. The outcome was by no means certain until late in the day when William gained the victory he needed following Harold's death in battle.

Word of Harold's victory at Stamford Bridge would be received in Filey with relief and, perhaps initially, events on the South Coast would seem to be too far away to be of any real consequence. However, if such were the case, the villagers of Filey, like many others, were soon to learn otherwise. It would not be long before bands of armed men speaking an unfamiliar tongue arrived in the district to make clear that they were now the masters; the Norman Conquest had indeed begun.

It was almost 20 years after William's victory that he decided, for reasons which are not fully understood, to set in motion the compiling of a full and detailed survey of the land of which he was King. It had not been an easy 20 years; many had not readily accepted William's sovereignty and he had spent much energy and time in quelling revolts, particularly in the North. After a second rising in 1069 had been put down, William wrought such havoc in Yorkshire as punishment that whole areas were depopulated with many inhabitants killed and dwellings destroyed.

The telling phrase *it is waste* occurs frequently in Domesday Book entries for Yorkshire.

The compilation of Domesday Book was a remarkable achievement and the survey is invaluable as a source material for those endeavouring to gain a picture of life in England soon after the Conquest.

Filey, or Fucelac as it is recorded in the Book, was perhaps the southernmost village in the Manor of Falsgrave. The uncertainty is because other Manor communities mentioned by name, for instance —*Eterstorp*, cannot be reliably identified. Other communities in the Manor included Staintondale, Wykeham and Lebberston.

Prior to the Conquest, Filey, being in the Manor of Falsgrave, belonged to Tosti (Tostig) who was the brother of King Harold. However, Tosti had rebelled against the King and sided with Harald Hardrada in an attempt to gain the throne for himself. In the battle of Stamford Bridge, Tosti died fighting valiantly soon after Harald Hardrada himself had been killed.

After the Conquest, William took the Manor of Falsgrave for himself, unlike many others which he gave to those who had come from Normandy with him. However, Filey soon passed into the Overlordship of the de Gants of Hunmanby.

An indication of the devastation wrought in the district by William's men is the telling phrase describing the Manor of Falsgrave — *Value before 1066: £56; now: 30/-*. Filey must have suffered cruelly and it is not hard to imagine roofless houses, an almost empty street, overgrown fields and fishing boats smashed beyond repair.

Clearly a scorched earth policy had been followed in the years prior to the Domesday survey, rendering the area around Scarborough one of the most severely treated in the North of England. The reason for this may be that in 1085, 16 years after the *Harrying of the North,* Cnut of Denmark was threatening to invade England with a large force and William ordered that nothing should be allowed to remain in coastal regions which might be of use to an invader.

William could not have benefited much from the concise information now at his disposal concerning the land and its people, for the survey was barely finished before his death in 1087. However, his son and successor, William II *Rufus,* no doubt made good use of this newly acquired information in his ceaseless search for revenue.

CHAPTER TWO

Medieval Village to Enclosed Township

Late - Medieval

After the devastation caused by William's harrying of the North soon after the Conquest, several years must have elapsed before the population level and the general living standard returned to what they had been in Edward the Confessor's day. In the early years of the 12th century, Filey must have been a primitive place with a bare subsistence existence for its few inhabitants. However, there must have been a gradual improvement for it was soon after this very difficult period that tithe disputes began. These indicate that Filey fishermen were accustomed to trips of several days duration. For these journeys substantial, sea-worthy vessels would be required and these could only be built by stable, organised communities.

Another indication that Filey was becoming an established community is that Richard of Hexham, in an account of the Battle of the Standard near Northallerton in 1138, describes Walter de Gant as being *of Filey*. A few years later, Walter's son Gilbert, gave to Thornton Abbey in Lincolnshire, a Filey house. There was also about this time a water-mill here, for in 1148 it was made a gift to St. Peter's Hospital, York.

A conclusive piece of evidence regarding the size and status of Filey at this time can be seen still, in the fine parish church of St. Oswald's. Begun in the late 12th century, its considerable size suggests very strongly that it was built for a fairly substantial community. Almost certainly there was a church in Filey prior to St. Oswald's for, about 1150, acting as a witness for a legal document was one, Randulph, described as being *Priest of Fithely*.

A right to hold a market is an issue still sometimes keenly contested and in medieval times such a right could be crucial to the economic health of a community and, if obtained, was jealously guarded. In 1221, Ralph de Neville was granted permission to hold a market on Fridays. Its position was probably where is now the junction of Scarborough Road, Station Road and Mitford Street. In 1231, Gilbert de Gant complained that Filey's market adversely affected his own market at Hunmanby and in 1256 even Scarborough weighed in with attempts to suppress Filey's market day. Its viability through the centuries is difficult to assess, but as late as the 1850s a Friday market for poultry and butter was being held. A market cross apparently stood at the aforementioned road-junction until the early 1800s when it was moved to the junction of Church Street and Queen Street. The cross subsequently disappeared.

Though we know so little of the inhabitants of those far-off days, personal names can be evocative and in the Chartularies of Bridlington Priory can be found references to Simon Dispenser, Robert the Steward and Robert the Chaplain they were men who lived here during the period when St. Oswald's was being built. Another name that calls across the years is that of Emera, described as the beautiful and religious daughter of Robert of Filey. She must also have been quite wealthy for she is described in 1219 as being a liberal benefactress of St. Mary's Hospital, Scarborough.

The sea was regarded as a provider of many things and there were therefore firm rules governing the ways in which they were shared out. An unusual rule was confirmed at Westminster in 1278, in the reign of Edward I, which stated that if a whale was washed up on Filey beach, Gilbert de Gant and Richard Malebysse were to share it, except for the head and tail which were the King's. How he was to take possession of them was not explained! The confirming of this right followed the inquisition at Filey on *Monday after the feast of St. Botulph* (20th June) before the Sheriff by eighteen *free and lawful men* who testified that the ancestors of the claimants had enjoyed this privilege.

Sovereigns have resorted to many methods of acquiring funds for campaigns, and in 1297 Edward I instituted a tax on all but the very poor, of a sum equal to one ninth of the total value of their possessions. No doubt this levy would be extremely unpopular, but the lay subsidy records provide us with the names of Filey's better-off householders; thirteen in number, their names were: Isabella Fauvel, Henrico ad Crucem (Henry Cross), Galfrido de Lebrestona, Petro filio Durandi, Durando, Simone filio Lucie, Simone Vapulatore, Ricardo de Cloftona, Johanne Cresk, Emma Berier, Waltero filio Lund, Thoma Carpentaria, and Galfrido de Abredene. Was the last named one of the first Scotsmen to settle in Filey?

Another name from the same period was recorded in less happy circumstances, and the reason for its recording indicates how harsh life could then be. In 1334, Will of Filey was outlawed for hunting hares in the Royal Forest of Pickering. There was nothing romantic in being an outlaw for there were few chances of long surviving such a sentence.

An indication of Filey's size in the 14th century is given by those records which number the poll tax payers. This tax was a more embracing form of raising revenue than the previously mentioned 1297 method. In 1377 in Filey, 165 were required to pay compared with nearly twice as many in Hunmanby.

Many small coastal communities regarded what might come to them as wreck of sea as a welcome addition to a sometimes spartan economy. Fortunately there is nothing to suggest that inhabitants were ever accused of deliberately causing a shipwreck, but if one occurred then advantage might be taken thereof.

The right to wrecks was a valuable one as shown by the petition of Lord of the Manor, Thomas Beckwith in 1447; inadvertently, the document confirming his inherited right to wreck had been burned and he found himself unable to prove his claim. However, his petition to Westminster was accepted and so once again he had first call on any wreck in Filey Bay.

According to Church records a chapel existed in, or near, Filey during these medieval years. Dedicated to St. Bartholomew, it was in ruins by 1567. A document of that year in the Beswick Family Collection refers to a grant by Francis Barker to William Lutton, Gent. of Filey, for a period, of a ruined chapel, St. Bartholomew's, and its grounds, in Filey.

Through the years of the times described as *Late Medieval* the 13th, 14th and 15th centuries, life in Filey continued to be centred on what is now Queen Street. In 1976, an excavation was carried out by members of the Filey Local History Society and the Scarborough Archaeological and Historical Society, under the direction of Peter Farmer. This took place on a site in Queen Street opposite to the Crown Hotel. The ground had recently been cleared in preparation for new buildings and in the short time available for the excavation, a considerable amount of pottery was unearthed and indications of several previous dwellings were revealed. The earliest period of occupancy of the site was seen to be 10th century with indications that families continued to live there through succeeding centuries. When the ground was first cleared two wells were revealed; one in a good state of preservation was shaped like a bottle and still contained water; surprisingly it had not been filled in when a 19th century shop had been erected over it.

There is no doubt that underneath many of the older buildings standing now in Queen Street there is much archaeological material and evidence of how early Filonians lived. Some of this will most probably be revealed in time to come.

Some of the stresses of late medieval life in Filey can be dimly discerned by the report that, in 1517, William Battom had taken possession of three houses with the consequence that 10 people had been evicted. Was this perhaps due to non-payment of rent, and where did these 10 new homeless go to find shelter, one wonders? A disadvantage of life in a fishing village a century later is indicated by the charge laid in 1622 at the Hunmanby Manor Court against three men that they threw fish guts in the street of Filey.

Filey through the years until the early 19th century was a mixed economy community with many of its men and women following a rural way of life common to thousands of villages throughout England. Much of their time would be spent in the open fields, ploughing and sowing the land and harvesting the crops. The plough oxen were kept in the Ox Close which was situated where is now the northern part of the Country Park. Filey apparently operated a three field rotation system in which, in any one year, two fields would be cultivated and the third would-recover some of its fertility by being allowed to remain fallow. The three fields were Church Field, Great Field and Little Field. The first is now much of the Country Park where there are still many clear examples of ridge and furrow cultivation. The Parish Fields estate, north of Scarborough Road, is built on what was Great Field, and Little Field was situated on both sides of West Avenue. This thoroughfare was first known as Little Field Road. Common land was an essential feature of a village economy and for Filonians it was mainly that part of the town inland of the line taken by the railway and to the north of Muston Road. Access to this area from the village was by Cottagers' Road, still known to some by its later name of Common Right. A later name was West Parade and the present one is West Road. Much of this common moor was wet land as it is still; however, in medieval times long before drainage took place, there was a considerable area of open water in which, in 1579, the Lord of Muston Manor had the fishing rights. No doubt, rights or not, fresh-water fish would provide a very welcome addition to the menu for many a Filey table. The name by which this area is still known, the Dams, recalls this time when several acres were under water.

It is an interesting exercise of imagination to attempt to visualise an early morning scene in say, 16th century Queen Street; those setting off for the open fields would perhaps meet and greet others making their way down to their boats drawn up on a part of the cliff secure from the sea. Remaining in Queen Street would be some of the craftsmen who were an essential part of a viable community. They would include perhaps, shoemakers, woodworkers, stonemasons and tailors. Although there is no indication that women, at any time, formed part of the crew of a fishing boat, they did perform an essential function in collecting bait, cleaning and baiting lines, and carrying lines to and fro' between bait-sheds and boats; all this was in addition to their usual household responsibilities. Women too carried out many of the tasks associated with work on the land.

In the time of Henry VIII and his daughters Mary and Elizabeth, religion was, for many, a dominant feature of everyday life. Henry's long-standing feud with the Roman Catholic Church created many dangers for both prominent and ordinary folk. One indication of the repression that existed is that in 1537, John Dobson, the Vicar of Muston, was executed at York because he had been heard in the local ale-house to speak well of the Pope but ill of the King! One of the acts for which Henry is remembered, the Dissolution of the Monasteries, provides us with one detail of life here then; in the same year that John Dobson lost his life, Bridlington Priory was dissolved and listed then amongst its possessions was a mill at *Fyveley* of value £1-4-0, though this 16th century sum has little meaning today.

Another order of Henry's, one which had a direct effect on the week-end activities of Filey's male population, was enacted some years earlier. With the intention of building up a military reserve for both defence and offence, Henry required all able-bodied men up to the age of 60, to practice archery after Sunday morning church service. Perhaps the timing explains why Filey's chosen site was between Ravine Hill and Church Hill, an open area known into this century as Butt Hills.

A few years only separated Henry's death in 1547 and the beginning of Elizabeth's reign in 1558, but in retrospect, associations with the two monarchs are for many so different that the period between represents the final ending of the long *Middle Ages*. Whether or not Elizabeth's time on the throne was a *Golden Age* we do feel closer in spirit to her life and times than to those of her father.

Filey's Landed Families

Prior to the Norman Conquest, Filey was part of the Manor of Falsgrave whose Lord was Tosti. In 1086 the six carucates of Filey land belonged still to the Falsgrave Manor, but they were now owned by King William. (A carucate was the amount of land which, it was estimated, could be cultivated by a team of eight oxen). Some time later Filey became part of the Manor of Hunmanby which was owned by the de Gants. The Hunmanby Manor was awarded, after the Conquest, by William to his nephew Gilbert de Gant (of Ghent in Belgium). Walter, Gilbert's son, founded Bridlington Priory and was given much of the credit for the victory of the English over the Scots at the Battle of the Standard near Northallerton in 1138. A later Gilbert de Gant played a major part in the revolt of the northern barons against King John in 1215 which led to the sealing of Magna Carta. After the de Gants, some of the estate was held by the Tattershalls by which time ownership of land in and around Filey was vested in several families. Amongst the names of such families were — Cockfield, Neville, Malbis, Beckwith, Maltby, Warton; and the St. Quintin family appear to have held land in Filey between the 14th and 16th centuries.

Although from the point of view of ownership of land, Filey could not now be regarded as part of the Manor of Hunmanby, nevertheless the lords of the manor there had considerable authority in Filey and held courts in Filey over a long period in the 16th and 17th centuries.

The Constable family held land in Filey from the 15th to 17th century. In 1775 the former Warton estates were divided and Michael Newton received a large part of Filey land, much of which he retained at Enclosure in 1791. The Osbaldestons of Hunmanby held land in Filey in the 18th century and the Osbaldeston-Mitfords were still local landowners in the early 20th century.

It is uncertain just when the Bucke family entered Filey's story and in particular just when their manor house to the north of St. Oswald's Church was built. Sir John Bucke was described as being *of Filey* when he was knighted at Whitehall in 1603. Perhaps Sir John was encouraged to live there by his wife

Elizabeth who was the daughter of William Greene of Filey. She outlived her husband by at least 20 years and presumably remained in Filey, for in 1668 she made her will, asking to be buried in the Quire of St. Oswald's Church. Members of their family apparently settled in other parts of the country, although in 1661 Lady Elizabeth's son and daughter-in-law, Sir John and Lady Mary Bucke, were active in trying to obtain for Filey a harbour of refuge.

Perhaps after Lady Bucke's death the manor house was no longer occupied. She was clearly a person of substance in Filey for she inherited from her father in 1605 the right to tithes which in 1650 brought her an income of £60 per year from Filey alone. The family retained much land, though living away from Filey until 1764, when Fountayne Wentworth Osbaldeston acquired it by purchase. Humphrey Osbaldeston subsequently obtained more Filey land and property in 1787 and consequently, at enclosure, he was allotted over 300 acres of Filey together with many buildings and some tithe-rents.

Although at enclosure patterns of land ownership changed considerably, it is perhaps surprising that Carr Naze was privately owned into the 20th century and the Lord of Hunmanby Manor still held rights over parts of the beach.

Sixteenth Century

England welcomed the accession of Elizabeth I in 1558 following five years of rule under Mary which saw the land divided and weakened as a result of Mary's attempts to restore the Catholic faith. Elizabeth's reign of more than forty years confirmed England in its Protestant faith and saw it much increased in strength and wealth. There was also an increase in literacy and the keeping of records of various kinds became more usual. Consequently it is possible now, by referring to parish records and muster rolls, to discover the names of many Elizabethan Filonians, to find out who was in the local defence force and how they prepared themselves to resist the Spanish Armada.

It is interesting to reflect that in the long list of events that might have been, there could be included a major sea battle off Filey. The circumstances were these; 130 ships of the Armada left Corunna in July 1558 and proceeded up the English Channel when the Spanish plans soon went very wrong. The intention had been to embark, in the Spanish Netherlands, the army of the Duke of Parma for the invasion of England, but the fire ships of Sir Francis Drake and defeat in a battle off Gravelines made this plan impossible to execute. The decision was taken to proceed north and the English Fleet followed in pursuit. In early August an English captain recorded how they followed the Spanish vessels as far as Flamborough Head by which time it was resolved to engage them again in battle. However, the engagement was called off when a check revealed that the Fleet was almost out of ammunition.

England had expected an invasion to take place and so prepared the means by which the country could rapidly be brought to arms. The early warning system of those days differed little in principle from that of the Romans 12 centuries earlier. One beacon blazing in a prominent position gave warning to observers stationed at another beacon a few miles away. Along the coast, fires were prepared at Bridlington and Flamborough amongst many others. Filey still has its Beacon Hill one half-mile west of Filey School, and as part of the warning system for the Armada the beacon there was prepared to take light from Reighton and give it to Staxton.

Filey was also prepared with its own 16th century Home Guard. The East Riding Muster Roll for Filey in 1584 names Reynold Furley as having a calever, and gives a total strength of 26, presumably all men (though Muston had one doughty woman, Dorothy Lacon, a widow who wielded a bow). Filey's men were archers, pikemen or billmen. The pike (up to 15 feet long) and the long bill were both effective against cavalry.

Instructions for the calever were daunting. It had a metre long barrel and in order to fire it, it was necessary to light a string soaked in saltpetre which was blown on to keep it glowing; the charge was rammed in followed by wads and a bullet. The pan was primed and the glowing string was so placed that when the trigger was pulled the powder on the pan was ignited. The flash passed through a touch-hole and caused the charge in the chamber to explode. One wonders how much less dangerous it was to be behind rather than in front of the gun!

It was seventeen years before the Spanish Armada set out when the Filey Parish Registers were begun. The first recorded marriage took place on the 14th June 1571 and was between Robert Smyth and Katherine Rickman. The first known baptism was that of John Clarke on 3rd January 1574 who was given his father's Christian name; it was not then thought necessary to record the mother's name! The first entry in the burial section is that of Will'm Cockrell who was buried on 17th May 1571.

Four hundred years of registers (with some breaks in continuity) provide a considerable amount of source material from which can be gained invaluable information about family names, occupations, community size and mortality rates. For instance, in the year of the Armada, 10 baptisms are recorded. In the same year there were apparently 7 weddings and 21 burials. The number of baptisms was lower than the average of 18 per year for the first 11 years of records. In order to obtain an estimate of population size, one perhaps may assume for late 16th century Filey, a life expectancy of about 42 years. This value leads to an estimated population of about 500. This figure is arrived at in the following way; the product of 42 and 18 is 756, but Gristhorpe and Lebberston were included in these records. The 1801 census gives the population numbers as 505 for Filey, 129 for Gristhorpe and 126 for Lebberston; a total of 760, almost exactly equal to the estimated value for the late 16th century. Comparison suggests therefore, perhaps surprisingly, that little population total change occurred in 200 years. This comparison does, of course, depend upon the reliability of the estimated value of life expectancy and the average number of births per year, also the constancy of the ratio of village sizes.

The Sixteenth Century ended only shortly before the long reign of Elizabeth came to a close with her death in 1603. To the throne came the son of Mary, Queen of Scots, James the Sixth of Scotland and First of England, who was to remain sovereign for the first quarter of the Seventeenth Century.

Seventeenth Century - Civil War

The 17th century had barely begun when Queen Elizabeth died, thus ending a remarkable reign of 45 years. The question that had frequently been asked during her later years of who would succeed her, was answered as James VI of Scotland made his way to London to become James I of England. Perhaps he chose the more arduous journey from Edinburgh by road rather than by sea so that he could see his new domain and be seen by his new subjects.

It is unlikely that the change of sovereign affected much the daily life of the 500 or so inhabitants of Filey. There was no great change in requirements of religious observance as there had been when Elizabeth succeeded Mary, and Scotland was too far away for the new accord between the two countries to be of much significance to the local community. However, there must have been resentment in the later years of James's reign as it became clear he was pursuing a weak maritime policy and life at sea was being made more difficult for both seamen and fishermen as the aggressive Dutch were not only ousting the English mariners from their trade routes, but driving English deep-sea fishermen from their traditional grounds and even taking large catches in inshore waters.

James was succeeded in 1625 by his son Charles I, but the quarrels between the new King and Parliament which soon began would not then seem of great importance several days journey away in Filey; that is until relations between the two seats of power, Throne and Parliament, broke down completely in the early 1640s.

The Great Civil War in the middle of the 17th century (1642-1646) was for many a devastating period, though there were those in England who remained relatively untouched by the battles, alarms and excursions of this unsettled time. The War saw shires, communities and even families divided; generally the aristocracy, the county squires and the cathedral towns supported the King, while sea-ports, clothing towns, London and the south favoured Parliament and Oliver Cromwell.

Much significant action occurred in places relatively close to Filey. It was the refusal of Sir John Hotham, as Governor of Hull, to allow Charles I to enter the city which brought to a head the tension between King and Parliament and thus began the War. Early in the War, forces in the Scarborough area were commanded by Sir Hugh Cholmley on behalf of Parliament, but in 1643 he changed sides and consequently Scarborough and East Yorkshire, except for

Hull, came under Royalist control for a time. Brian Beswick of Gristhorpe served as an officer in the Royalist garrison at Scarborough Castle, as also did Sir Michael Warton of Muston, who died of wounds received there during an attack by the Parliamentary Army.

Also in 1643, Henrietta Maria, Charles's Queen and daughter of Henry IV of France, landed at Bridlington with troops en route to join the King's Army at York. Soon after landing, Bridlington was bombarded by the ships of the Parliamentary fleet and it is said the Queen took cover by the Gypsey Race. At Boynton Hall she left her portrait in exchange for family plate and then stayed overnight at Burton Fleming.

In 1645, after a long and bitter siege, Scarborough Castle was finally taken by Parliamentary forces and a National Day of Thanksgiving was declared on 19th August. The reason for this was that the Royalist garrison had controlled shipping in and out of the harbour and armed vessels based there had so disrupted the carriage of coal to London that the citizens had experienced real deprivation. No doubt some Filonians would be witnesses to the fierce battles at the Castle and the sounds of cannon fire would often be heard here.

The Parliamentary soldiery had in many places a reputation for unruly behaviour which would be experienced here though records are minimal. William Beswick of Gristhorpe refers in his diary to recollections of older family members who found it necessary to move from Muston because of plundering parties of soldiers from Cromwell's army. At one stage of the conflict, Filey's Lord of the Manor, Sir John Bucke, commanded a company, no doubt containing Filey men, in Sir Matthew Boynton's Regiment on the side of Parliament.

The names of some Parliamentary soldiers quartered locally are known from Civil War billeting papers. Lt. Col. Goodricke and Capt. Todde stayed in Hunmanby, Sgt. Jessop was billeted there at the home of Francis Worfolke for three weeks and Cpl. Moore stayed with Joseph Leppington. Regrettably, it appears six soldiers of Capt. Bacon's Company left the same village owing the sum of £1-7-0 for accommodation.

The confusion often inherent in civil wars in which there is no clear battle line is indicated by the message sent by the Royalist Lord Digby in August 1645 which asked for gunpowder to be sent by ship to Whitby or Bridlington *for Scarborough is lost, but enquire before putting in, in case the enemy have garrisoned these places.* One wonders if the answer to the enquiry might have been an explosive one!

The Civil War finally drew to a close with the execution of Charles I and the assumption of power by Parliament and Oliver Cromwell.

However, the Yorkshire coast was still a dangerous sea-way for shipping in the 1650s. Charles II (son of Charles I) was in exile on the continent but was able to commission vessels from Holland and elsewhere to carry on the battle against Parliament. The English were at war with the Dutch in the years 1652-4 and in February 1652 pickeroons hid behind Flamborough Head in order to surprise vessels sailing south across Filey Bay. In April 1653 a battle fleet of 20 Dutch ships caused a convoy of colliers to take refuge in Scarborough Harbour. The Hollanders had been observed off Flamborough Head on the 5th sailing north; on reaching Scarborough they exchanged shots with the Castle battery but decided there was little purpose in staying in the area and soon sailed back down the coast and out of sight to the great relief of Scarborough and the colliers' crews.

Filey's population remained relatively small through the centuries. Hearth tax returns were prepared as the means by which those families who could afford to pay tax might be identified. The returns for 1672 indicate that there were 77 households in Filey in that year representing a population perhaps of about 400. Two years later it was reported that only 9 households had two or more hearths; a statistic that indicates that Filey was not a prosperous community.

The later years of the 17th century were relatively peaceful with memories of the Civil War becoming ever more faint. The pattern of life in Filey with its dependence on fishing and tilling the soil would be little changed from earlier times. Perhaps a little more education was available for the sons of one or two local families and some rather more substantial houses were being built, a few of which still stand, even if somewhat altered.

Eighteenth Century

The Eighteenth Century could be described as the Century of the Georges. After Queen Anne died in 1714 she was succeeded by the first George who reigned until 1727, then the second who was King until 1760, and finally George III saw out the century, and in fact the first twenty years of the Nineteenth Century.

Events internationally were, in the main, to do with complex European politics, the opening of trade routes and the building of Empire. At the same time the structure of society was changing quite rapidly with the so-called Industrial Revolution beginning to gain momentum. In the middle years, the Jacobite challenge, which brought 5,000 armed Highlanders, almost unopposed as far south as Derby, exposed the social instability in the nation.

However for most of the hundred or so Filey families these events took place too far away to be really important. Certainly for many local people the undercover activities of smugglers of contraband would be of more interest and of more concern.

Filey for most of this century remained a fairly closed community; the coast road by-passed the village and few would venture here except to do business. However towards the end of the century a few visitors did make the journey here from Scarborough to walk or ride on the beach, some of whom would find accommodation in private homes,

In the last quarter of the century, two significant events took place within a few years of each other. One, the battle in Filey Bay would be talked about through much of Europe and North America, but had little real effect on the local community; the other, the Enclosure Award, would hardly be spoken of outside the village but it resulted in a major change in the lives of many of the inhabitants.

John Paul Jones

5. John Paul Jones's ship the *Bonhomme Richard* is pictured in battle with the British ship *Serapis* on September 23, 1779.

It is a surprising fact of history that the naval battle described as the bloodiest of the American War of Independence was fought in Filey Bay.

The circumstances were these — In 1779, John Paul Jones at the age of 32, was in command of the vessel *Bonhomme Richard* in the service of the American Colonies in their fight for independence. Born in Scotland, he had gone to sea when 12 years old but later found himself in trouble with the authorities and moved to Virginia in 1773. Jones joined the American Navy, newly formed by Congress, on the outbreak of war in 1775. Two years later he was given command of the frigate *Ranger* with a commission to 'distress the enemies of the United States', and in April 1778 he raided the port of

Whitehaven on the Solway Firth. In spite of his effectiveness as a raider he was deprived of his command, but some time later while in France, acquired with French help, another vessel which he named the *Bonhomme Richard.* In the summer of 1779 he sailed with four other vessels to wreak what havoc he could around the British coast.

On September 23rd, the squadron under Jones' command sailed out from its position just south of Flamborough Head to attack a convoy of merchantmen under escort by the British naval vessels *Serapis* and *Countess of Scarborough.* As the merchant vessels scattered battle was engaged by the seven armed vessels. The *Bonhomme Richard,* and the *Serapis,* under Captain Richard Pearson, were soon locked in combat while the American frigate *Alliance* under its eccentric Captain Landais circled the protagonists pouring shot indiscriminately into both ships!

It was at this point that Pearson challenged Jones to surrender, only to receive the legendary reply 'I have not yet begun to fight!' — a response quoted many times since aboard fighting ships of the United States Navy.

The battle continued with the *Serapis* and the *Bonhomme Richard* firing into each other at point-blank range until the turning point came when an intrepid sailor made his way to the end of the main yard-arm of the *Bonhomme Richard* with a bucket loaded with grenades which he dropped one by one down the main hatch-way of the *Serapis* causing a disabling explosion on the gun deck. It was thus Captain Pearson who soon after was to surrender, to the relief of Paul Jones whose own vessel was clearly foundering. Transferring his flag to the *Serapis,* Jones returned to France after unsuccessfully trying to save his own ship which later sank off Flamborough Head.

Jones received a great welcome from the French and later the thanks of Congress together with the congratulations of George Washington. Pearson was knighted for his valiant fight and for his success in saving the merchant vessels from the marauders.

The battle, fought on a clear moonlit night, was watched by hundreds of spectators from the cliffs. The combatants were so close in that several cannon balls struck the cliffs near to the observers. After the battle, seven unwilling members of Jones' crew, sailors who had been pressed into service after being captured and taken to France, escaped by boat and having reached the shore at Filey were taken before Humphrey Osbaldeston, J.P., of Hunmanby, to relate their experiences.

Many attempts to find the wreckage of the flagship of the man sometimes described as the *Father of the American Navy* have been made; the most determined of which was in the late 1970s in the hope that something might be found in time for the bicentenary in 1979 of the battle. This search was carried out on behalf of the United States Navy, the National Ocean Industries Association and the Atlantic Charter Maritime Archaeological Foundation.

However, nothing that could definitely be identified as being from John Paul Jones' ship was found. Local divers still continue the search.

After the war, Jones left the American service, became an Admiral in the Russian Navy, and eventually died in Paris in 1792.

The 18th Century – Enclosure

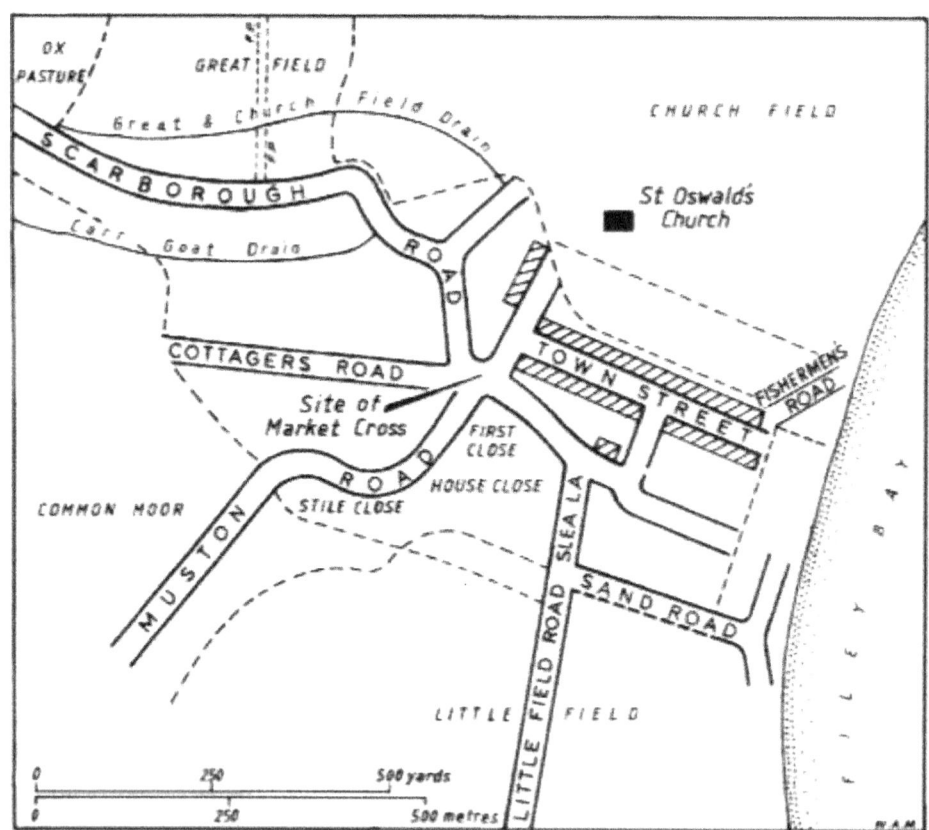

6. Filey in Pre-enclosure Days.

As it was similarly for many communities in England, almost certainly the most significant event in the 1700s for Filey was the passing in Parliament of 'An Act for Dividing, Allotting and Inclosing the Several Open and Common Arable Fields, Meadows, Pastures, Commons and Waste Grounds within the Township of Filey, otherwise Filo in the East and North Ridings of the County of York'.

This Act, as the document was endorsed, 'in the 28th year of the reign of George the Third' resulted in the appointing of Commissioners who carried out the requirements of the Act by producing the Filey Award which was enrolled at the Public Register Office at Beverley in December 1791.

In order to appreciate the importance of this Award, it is necessary to consider the way in which the land in the Filey Parish had previously been husbanded. Through the Middle Ages the usual system throughout England was for the land worked by a village community to be divided into strips. The strips were aggregated into two, three or four Fields and a rotation system was employed to allow each Field to lay fallow every two, three or four years. The strips were owned or tenanted by the villagers. The divisions of the strips varied considerably, but would be about a furlong (furrow long), i.e. 220 yards, in length and a few yards wide. The Country Park retains clear indications of strip farming as does the Miniature Golf Course, and also part of the Glen Gardens.

In Filey the three fields system was employed and the fields were named Great Field, Church Field and Little Field. Church Field was to the north of St. Oswald's where is now the Country Park; Great Field was the land on which are now built the new estates north of Scarborough Road, and Little Field occupied both sides of Little Field Road, now known as West Avenue.

Although the Field System was reasonably fair in that it enabled the good and the poor land to be shared, it was clearly very inefficient. The process of enclosure and re-distribution took place throughout England during several centuries; sometimes it was by agreement, but often by Act of Parliament. In the East Riding, Scagglethorpe was the first township to be enclosed by Act and this took place in 1725. Most enclosure occurred in the periods 1760-80 and 1790-1815.

The actual re-distribution of the land was carried out by Commissioners appointed under the Act. For Filey they were Isaac Leatham of Barton-le-Street; John Ford of Ayton; and John Wood of North Cave. The township had previously been surveyed by Joseph Dickenson who calculated the area of open land as being 695 acres, 1 rood, 12 perches, and the already enclosed land as containing 66 acres, 0 roods, 10 perches. Bearing in mind a perch is about 30 square yards this is a commendably precise assessment, especially considering the possible sudden changes due to coastal erosion.

It is interesting to note that both Isaac Leatham and Joseph Dickenson were Quakers. Possibly they were chosen because of the known reputation of Quakers to be scrupulously fair and honest in their dealings.

In addition to re-distributing the arable land the opportunity was also taken to establish an adequate road system in and around the town with widened main highways. These included Muston Road, Scarborough Road, Sand Road (now Murray Street), Great Carr Goat Road (now Ravine Hill) and Cottagers' Road (now West Road as far as the Junior School). Close attention was also given to the provision of a much improved drainage system, though these were for the most part surface drains.

Those who acquired the greatest allotments under the re-distribution of land were Humphrey Osbaldeston with 376 acres, Michael Newton who received 122 acres, and Christopher Foster, 101 acres. Other recipients included Thomas Robinson with 15 acres, Robert Rowe with 16 acres, and Elizabeth Huntress who received 8 acres.

The establishment of clear titles to substantial pieces of land in and around the town made the processes of sale and purchase much more convenient to conduct, and this was a major factor in the ease with which land was soon to be acquired for housing for residents new to Filey.

How valued today would be a contemporary, first hand account of everyday life, in pre-enclosure Filey. Apparently, to our loss, no diarist's notes, if compiled, survive and no traveller passed through and recorded his impressions. We can therefore only surmise and, in so doing, base our imaginings on what is known of similar communities elsewhere in the land.

CHAPTER THREE

The Victorians Build a New Town

Nineteenth Century

Filey entered the Nineteenth Century with its inhabitants still adjusting to the radical changes in its structure occasioned by Enclosure. The number of inhabitants in 1801 we know accurately as this was the year of the first of the ten-year interval census returns. It was then recorded that 505 people were living here, a figure which, when compared with estimates from previous times, suggests that there had been little population change for perhaps three centuries. The next decade saw an increase of 16% and during the following ten-year interval the number of inhabitants rose by 33% to a total of 773; the development of Filey was under way. This increase was certainly due, in part, to new people taking up residence here, but perhaps due more to the improved living standards which, nationally, resulted in a doubling of the population during the sixty years reign of George III. In the 1830s new building contributed to a population increase to 1,231 by 1841.

An indication of the interest now being taken in Filey as a community is given by the support shown in 1823 by residents of Scarborough, York and Hull in the establishment of a lifeboat station here.

In 1820, George III was succeeded by the fourth George. In spite of being somewhat unpopular because of the unsavoury manner in which he had instituted divorce proceedings against Queen Caroline, when in the royal yacht he passed Filey on Monday 12th August 1822 on his way to Edinburgh, Lady Murray erected a tent on Carr Naze near the Spa for herself and her friends.

George IV reigned for ten years to be succeeded by his more liked and respected brother, William IV. As William was then nearly sixty-five years old his reign was a short one of seven years. The next two sovereigns were to do what only one previous monarch — Elizabeth — had done, that is to bestow their names each upon an era. Victoria's time upon the throne was one of great change for Filey, as it was indeed for the country as a whole.

Victorian Filey

When the plan for New Filey was prepared in 1835 by Charles Edge, Architect and Surveyor of Birmingham, on the instructions of John Wilkes

7. A busy day in the Bay in Filey's very early days as a holiday resort.

Unett, William IV was on the throne. The reign of Queen Victoria, begun two years later, was to see Filey changed from a fishing and farming village with a very few new villas, into a town still containing a fishing community of significance, but one now known widely as a substantial resort with an enviable reputation

In 1837 the population of Filey was about 1000 (800 in 1831 and 1230 in 1841), almost all of whom were living in or near to Queen Street. About ten years had still to elapse before the arrival of the railway, and those wishing to come to, or leave Filey, would do so by boat, on foot, on horseback or by horse-drawn vehicle. Stage-coaches ran between Scarborough and Hull calling at Filey and providing a regular but very infrequent service. One of the first public buildings of the Victorian era was the Methodist Church in Murray Street which opened in 1838 and which became the Victoria Hall when the Methodists moved to Trinity Church nearly 40 years later. For the convenience of residents of and visitors to New Filey, the Church of England Iron Church was built in West Avenue in 1857 and used until superseded by St. John's Church in 1871.

In the earliest Victorian days, inns were almost the only place of entertainment. These included the Ship, now a private house; the Packhorse (replaced by the Crown Hotel in 1877); the Britannia, also in Queen Street (closed in February 1888); and the Hope and Anchor in Church Street. The Hotel in Queen Street owned by Mr. Thomas Foord was amongst the first establishments built to provide accommodation for visitors.

Hunmanby was the post town for Filey — its population in 1837 was almost exactly equal to that of Filey.

The earliest days of Victoria's reign saw the establishment of the small estate of Ravine Villa by Henry Bentley (of Bentley's Yorkshire Brewery). It included the ravine (then known as Bentley's Gill), in which was built an underground ice house, and the grounds now known as Glen Gardens. The house was Georgian in style with a five-bay front, a Greek Doric porch and balustrade. The lodge in West Avenue still stands.

In the early 1850s the Filey Gas Company was established to bring to the inhabitants the ease and convenience of cooking and lighting by gas. This facility, now taken so much for granted, must then have seemed a minor miracle. Another utility company, the Filey Waterworks Company, came into being in 1856 and supplied homes with piped water. This too must have proved a real boon to those who previously had to rely on water from deep well or Church Ravine spring. (When old property in Queen Street was demolished in the 1970s to prepare for the new development opposite the Crown Hotel, a brick-lined well was discovered over which had stood a shop for many years). Three years later the Gas Company was taken over by the Water Company.

The establishment of the Local Board of Health in 1868 was an important event. It was the forerunner of the Filey Urban District Council and took over the responsibilities of the Nuisance Removal Committee established in

8.. Built in 1857 the Filey Methodist Day School served the community until 1908. The building is now Dixon's T.V. Store.

1855, and which was aptly named! Some of the problems facing both committee and board were concerned with the traditions of disposing of rubbish by throwing it into Church Ravine and allowing raw sewage to run down on to the beach. The laying of drains in 1857 improved matters considerably. A storm in the same year resulted in a rush of water down Church Ravine which badly damaged the stone bridge leading to the Church. In 1869, the Local Board bought the land in and around the Ravine and instituted a competition with prizes of £25 and £10, for plans to lay out the Ravine as a park with trees, shrubs and foot paths.

Two years later the necessary work, which included culverting the stream, had been completed. Many of the paths are still in being on the Ravine sides though are now little used.

About this time a Telegraph Service was established and a Medical Officer of Health appointed. An indication of the hardships that resulted from a poor winter's fishing is the establishment in 1867 of a soup kitchen. Such charitable endeavours were found to be necessary for many years to come. In 1892, 60 gallons were consumed twice a week in the Ebenezer Methodist Church Schoolroom.

The increasing importance of leisure activities in the lives of many of the residents is indicated by the founding in 1886 of both a Tennis Club and a Debating Society: the Club's activities centred on the Tennis Courts and Croquet Lawn which had recently been established behind the Crescent Hotel.

Coastal erosion was always a matter of concern, and in 1889 in order to protect his recently acquired estate, Edwin Martin caused to be built the wooden defence work which became known to succeeding generations as Martin's Barrier. These defences were substantial and well constructed and performed the purpose for which they were intended until damaged beyond repair by the devastating storm of early 1953.

The increase in size and importance of Filey as a community is indicated by the acquisition of a fire engine in February 1891, and the building of the Police Station in Murray Street in 1892. By 1900 the engine was housed in Queen Street. In January 1895, under the Local Government Act of 1894, the Local Board became the Filey Urban District Council with nine members and by 1898 was using newly built offices in Queen Street.

The acquisition of a fire-engine in early 1891 is perhaps not unconnected with the serious fire in October 1890 which at one stage threatened to destroy the most northern block of Crescent houses (numbers 1-7). The outbreak occurred in a furniture store behind number 7 and soon spread to adjoining stables and shops. The three-storey shop and store were burnt to the ground and this might also have been the fate of several Crescent houses but for the intervention of a team of fishermen, led by Matthew (Walsher) Jenkinson, who climbed on the roofs and kept the flames at bay with a steady supply of buckets of water. A major concern was the non-appearance of the fire-engine

9. Clearly seen in this 1880s view of the sea-front are two boat-building yards and the primitive sea defences.

which eventually arrived four and a half hours after the fire began! Even bearing in mind that the engine may have had to come from Scarborough, the scathing comments of the amateur fire-fighters are understandable. The Filey Post reporter was clearly unimpressed by the 'crowds of people' from Scarborough who, he said '....poured down from the station off the 2.54 train expecting to see the best part of poor little Filey in ruins, and loud were the expressions of disappointment by them on beholding that not a single house on the Crescent was burnt'.

The fire was eventually brought under control, due in part to the residents and visitors (including 'several ladies, who worked hard and put several men into the shade') who formed lines to carry buckets of water to the seat of the fire.

Another indication of the increasing provision of leisure activities was the opening of a golf course on 19th August 1897 where the Country Park now is. However, satisfactory permanent arrangements between the Club and landowner could not be reached and two years later the Golf Club moved to its present position.

Before the introduction of the National Health Service, a concern for many was how, in the event of illness, medical expenses might be met. One way to relieve, at least partly, this anxiety was to join a Friendly Society. In addition to the simple health insurance provided for a small subscription there were also the joys of eagerly awaited anniversary celebrations which included a procession through the town wearing the appropriate sash, a special church service and a convivial meal at a local hostelry. Filey's societies included the Ravine Lodge of Loyal and Independent Oddfellows founded in 1838 — in 1875, 300 gathered for their anniversary celebrations in a marquee behind the Ship Inn! The Hollon Lodge of the same Order began in 1864 and had 82 members in 1882. The Mitford Lodge of Free and Independent Shepherds was constituted in 1861 and when they marched the members wore green sashes and carried sticks with small brass shepherds' crooks. In 1868 another society was formed — the Ancient Order of Foresters. The introduction of free medical treatment led to the demise of many such societies including the Ravine Lodge of Oddfellows which ended over a century of welfare work in 1949.

Even by the end of Victoria's reign conditions for working men left much to be desired as indicated by the labourers' strike in Filey in May 1900. After taking into account the changes in monetary values, the demand for 5½d per hour still seems modest enough! However, the offer of 5d only led to the labourers' withdrawal of labour.

In the days of long before Radio York and before local evening papers, the main method by which news of interest to the community could be quickly disseminated was the employment of a Town Crier. In Filey, that position was occupied for many years by Robert Stork who would announce concerts, meetings and shows as well as acting as a lost and found agency and arranging,

10. A valued study of the craftsmen who built the Ebenezer Methodist Chapel; it opened in June 1871.

11. The Filey section of the East Yorkshire Artillery Volunteers about 1898.

in a stentorian voice, assignations between anonymous young ladies and gentlemen. One wonders how many hopefuls turned up after hearing 'A gentleman wishes to meet a certain lady in Church Ravine at 7 o'clock....' Robert Stork obviously enjoyed his role, for in March 1902 he was appointed for his 28th year in office in spite of having just celebrated his 80th birthday.

The unsettled state of European politics in Victoria's time meant that the defence of the realm was always a pre-occupation, and Filey, like most communities of sufficient size, had a voluntary military unit. In January 1867 at the banquet given at the Foords Hotel by Sir Charles Legard to the 2nd East Yorkshire Artillery Volunteers, 80 guests were present, nearly all of whom were in full uniform; a fine sight they must have made. The adjutant, Captain Symonds, V.C., had occasion to express regret that the corps had been unable to use their 32-pounder gun for several months. The reason was that Mr. Bentley of Ravine Villa had complained to the Secretary of State that his visitors were disturbed by the gun firing out to sea from its emplacement on the cliff. However, the Secretary eventually rejected the complaint and the Volunteers resumed their gunnery practice.

The development of an extensive railway system enabled large travelling shows to move around the country. One of the largest such shows was Foottit's Great Allied Circus which visited Filey in May 1874 when it brought 80 horses and 50 artists. A rather more modest form of entertainment was that provided by the roller-skating rink which opened in John Street in the mid 1870s.

Grand occasions were eagerly anticipated and talked about for long afterwards. The participants would sometimes require considerable stamina as would the 200 revellers who attended the Ball at the Spa Saloon in 1884 where the dancing began at 9.30 p.m. and went on to 6.00 a.m! Fancy Dress Balls were also joyful and energetic occasions like one held on 9th January 1901 at the Victoria Hall. As the local press reported — 'Dancing began at half-past eight and was kept up with much spirit until half-past three next morning'.

Late Victorian joys, which residents and visitors could share in, were the performances of Mr. F. R. Benson's Shakespearean Company in Ravine Villa grounds. These included *As You Like It* in 1898, *Twelfth Night* in 1899 and in 1900 *Much Ado About Nothing,* a startling performance in that the stage gave way during the first act! Fortunately no-one was hurt.

An unusual event occurred in March 1876 when the Staintondale Hunt met at the Grapes Inn. The huntsmen and hounds arrived in the evening and the riders enjoyed a 'splendid dinner provided by Mr. Smith, the landlord'. The following morning a large crowd assembled to see them start from Church Cliff Farm and head towards Gristhorpe. Entertainment of a different type was provided in September 1879 by 'Fred French's Clouds and Sunshine Musical Entertainment' at the Spa Saloon, and in October by C. Baylis's Far Famed Marionettes. Admission was 2s, 1s and 6d; children and servants half price.

12. A print published by Rock and Co in January 1872.

13. In the 1880s a boat builder's premises stood on the present day Deepdene site.

A popular annual event was the Filey Floral, Horticultural, Horse, Dog, Cat and Poultry Show. The total value of the prizes at the tenth show in August 1881 was £150, a very considerable sum for the time. However, at the luncheon, when Sir Charles Legard was proposing a toast to the show's organisers, he happened in passing to refer to 'free trade policy'. This produced a protest at politics being introduced and uproar followed with protests, cheers and counter-cheers. Politics were taken seriously then.

Amateur entertainment in the form of Spelling Bees were popular about the same time and were highly organised with intense competition for the prizes.

Outdoor sporting events were also popular; the Sailing Race and Athletic Sports held in September 1890 was just such an occasion. The sailing race was for local fishing-boats for which the Earl of Ranfurly was judge and handicapper; the sports took place on the beach and included a wheelbarrow race with lady passengers, a floating tub and shovel race, a sack race, and a head-over-heels competition. Perhaps the Victorians weren't so serious after all!

Serious or not, decorum had to be preserved even on the beach or in the water. Bathing machines were small wooden huts on wheels designed to enable bathers to change and step straight down into the water. In 1878 the Local Board's Bye-Law No.164 required a minimum distance of 130 feet between 'any machine containing a male or males and one containing a female or females'!

By the end of Victoria's reign the distinctions between Old Filey and New Filey were becoming blurred, although some residents of either part could still live out their lives and seldom have occasion to cross the hypothetical boundary which would be somewhere in the vicinity of Murray Street. A major factor in this separate existence was that well into the 20th century, Queen Street alone had more than 20 shops covering a wide range of goods, although by then the main shopping and business area of Filey was as it is now.

The final two years of Victoria's reign were overshadowed by the Boer War. Although this was a relatively small conflict by comparison with the two World Wars which were to follow, intense patriotic fervour was generated by it. The events of the War were closely followed and there was jubilation when it was finally over. In June 1902 local congregations leaving Sunday evening services heard the glad tidings as newsboys shouted 'Peace Proclaimed'. Several Filey men made the long voyage to South Africa and in November 1901 those still at the front were: William Jenkinson, 18th Hussars; Richard Barker, East Kent Buffs; Herbert Gardner, Yorkshire Yeomanry; George Mallinson and Edward Perryman, South African Constabulary; and John Harrison, Princess of Wales Own Yorkshire Regiment. Casualties of the war were: T. Scott of Grove Villa and S. Cappleman, who died respectively of enteric fever and dysentery. Herbert Gardner had both a stirring send-off and reception; he was played to the railway station by Filey Brass Band in February 1901, and on his return in September 1902 was drawn in a carriage round Filey by his friends, preceded by the Brass Band. Another South African veteran was Charles Smith of Church Farm for whom a reception was organised in September 1901 at the Victoria Hall. In July of the previous year he had seen the Maxim gun given to the expeditionary force by Miss Clarke of Northcliffe and named *The Elinor* in her honour!

So began the 20th Century with a new monarch and the ending of a debilitating war. Filonians, like so many others, began the process of adjusting to life without the Queen whose reign had lasted for an astonishing 63 years.

A Slightly Tarnished Image

With justification Filey has over the years acquired the image of a rather *select* resort. There have, however, been occasions when that image has been a little tarnished! The Filonian on learning of this may be somewhat relieved to hear that the blame usually lay outside the town!

One such occasion was in April 1882 when, early in the evening, the local police arrested two men for being 'drunk and disorderly'. This action led to the policemen being subjected to a barrage of glass bottles, bricks, sticks and stones thrown by companions of the arrested men. The scale of the assault may be judged from the report to the court of P.C. Chambers who estimated at 150 the number of men who poured out of a hostelry in Queen Street! The rear-guard action fought by the police as they made their hazardous way to the Police Station must, for many, have changed for a long time the idea of Filey as a quiet peaceful little place! The outcome of this incident was that 12 men, mainly from Scarborough, and 1 woman, were charged, with sentences of several months imprisonment with hard labour being imposed.

In September 1910 a similar situation developed in Murray Street when a crowd estimated to be about 100 strong gathered round Superintendent Escrick as he attempted to stop fighting which had broken out late at night outside the Three Tuns. Although the crowd was described as being hostile, prompt action apparently was effective and the only sentence was a fine of 5s.

Offences involving property were severely regarded by the Victorians, as is shown by the sentence handed out locally in February 1872 to 15-year old Caroline Coleman for stealing a 5s telescope. She was sentenced to 3 months hard labour and three years in a reformatory.

Two charges seldom appearing in court lists today were made in 1891, when John Bennett was said to have driven a cow on the footpath and George Ingamells had surreptitiously changed the name of Station Road to Muston Road!

In 1895, Henry Gage, a groom, was fined £1-5s-0d, a sum probably equivalent to a week's wage, for furiously riding his bicycle on the Crescent — at 10 to 15 mph! A few months later, in June 1896, Nelson Barnes a cabinet

14. Queen Street about 1900.

maker, was a little more fortunate; he was fined only 10s for the same offence of 'riding his bicycle in a furious manner' on the Crescent.

Incidents of wilful damage to property and complaints about litter were certainly not unknown in late Victorian days; in April 1899 protests were made concerning the £20 worth of broken tiles in the Foreshore shelters and also the amount of rubbish that was being thrown down the banks into Church Ravine.

An outbreak of stone-throwing seems to have swept over Filey in December 1900 when a postman was fined for bombarding telegraph poles in this way, and fines were also imposed on two other men for throwing stones at an old man on the Coble Landing. In September 1905 an offence entirely absent from today's Court Lists brought a 2s.6d fine for the defendant who had allowed seven of his pigs to stray in West Street (now West Avenue).

In April 1881 there took place what must at the time have seemed to be little short of an invasion of the town. Not, as has been feared on many occasions, from the sea, but from Scarborough. The invaders arrived in the afternoon in 36 cabs and a waggonette and were described as fisher lads and lasses, the majority of whom were intoxicated, many of them in their early teens. On arrival they 'to a great extent took possession of the town and rioted about in a most disgraceful manner until eleven o'clock at night'. Surprisingly, in view of the apparent seriousness of the situation, the only sentences awarded were two fines, each of £1.

An incident in a lighter vein took place in November 1882 when two local men were charged with riotous conduct. Their offence took place at the Albert Hall and was in talking aloud and making people laugh while William Clarke of the United Christian Army was reading the lesson. This shocking behaviour, coupled with the struggles at the door that followed, led to fines of £1 and 10s. (The Albert Hall was the former Bethesda Methodist Chapel and stood where the Salvation Army Hall is now).

Filey today resembles many similarly-sized communities in that most offences that are committed here are associated with the motor-car. A road system developed for relatively few horse-drawn vehicles has to cope with the hundreds of locally owned motor vehicles and the thousands that are brought into the town in the Season. In spite of the number of fines imposed for motoring offences some credit must be given to those responsible for road maintenance and traffic movement that the great majority of road users go about their business with little delay and few difficulties.

The Sea Wall And Promenade

By far the most ambitious scheme carried through either by Filey Town Council or its predecessors was the one which resulted in the Sea Wall and Promenade.

15. For a hundred years the Crescent Hotel was one of Britain's leading hotels.

In earlier years there had been constructed sea defence works, particularly between Carr Gate Hill and Crescent Hill, but as photographs indicate, these had been much smaller in scale.

That there were those prepared to build such impressive buildings as the Ackworth and Downcliffe so close to the water with so little defence is a matter of some surprise. However, by the late 1880s it was clear to many that a major work was increasingly necessary.

Early hopes had centred on the possibility of a harbour scheme, but by 1885 it was apparent that no such scheme was likely to come to fruition. Informal and formal discussions took place and an early encouraging offer was that made by the Lord of the Manor, Colonel Mitford of Hunmanby Hall, in February 1892, to make available stone from the Brigg at one farthing (about 0.1p) per ton.

In October 1891, Mr. Graham Fairbank of Fairbank and Son, of Driffield and Westminster, was appointed by the local Board as Engineer. Financial support of £300 was promised by the Admiralty; no doubt because it would be an advantage to the Coastguards. Soon, tenders were called for and when received found to range between £10,955 and £15,046. The lowest was accepted but then withdrawn by the contractor. Eventually the tender of James Dickson of St. Albans was accepted and loans totalling £12,000, mainly from the Ecclesiastical Commissioners, obtained.

At a public meeting in July 1892 the opinion was expressed that the project was too large in concept and a wooden barrier would be more appropriate; however, in spite of this objection the scheme went ahead.

In October work began with the delivery of cement and the laying of a railway along the beach to the Brigg along which stone could be brought. The first block was laid on 24th April 1893 by Mrs. Edwin Martin of Ravine Hall and subsequent progress was rapid. The trowel and mallet used by Mrs. Martin are in the possession of the Town Council. The number of men employed was usually more than two hundred who, in addition to having their own missionary, also had classes and entertainment arranged by two local ladies, Miss Pym and Miss Brown. It was calculated that 40,000 cubic yards of material were used to infill behind the wall.

The Wall was completed in the early summer of 1894 and it then had a double flight of iron steps in the centre of each section. The opening ceremony was performed on the 19th June, on the bridge in the centre of the Promenade, by Lord Herries in his capacity of Lord Lieutenant of the East Riding.

On the following Sunday, the Vicar, the Rev. A.N. Cooper, preached appropriately from the text, Nehemiah 6.15, "...the wall was finished".

Credit must be given to the farsightedness of the members of the Local Board who overcame many difficulties to bring into being a sea defence work which has fulfilled its purpose admirably now for one hundred years and fourteen years.

It has also made a major contribution to the attractiveness of Filey for residents and visitors alike. The high standards employed in its construction are indicated by the fact that relatively little maintenance has been required in that long time.

CHAPTER FOUR

Peace and War

Twentieth Century

We know more about the Twentieth Century than about all previous centuries taken together. This is because it is the one which, by far, has been the most documented and recorded. The two World Wars enable the Century to be divided logically into five sections.

Edwardian Filey

Many communities have a period in their histories to which residents look back almost with a feeling of nostalgia, even if such a period was not part of their own experience. For Filey, this time was those few years between the end of the Boer War and the beginning of World War I. That this is so is confirmed by the enthusiasm with which Filonians welcomed and supported in recent years the Edwardian Festival.

Why is this period so special in the minds of residents of Filey? Of several possible reasons two at least applied nationally. The Boer War caused much distress, and its end was welcomed with relief; the years preceding the First World War were generally peaceful and have been looked back upon by people caught up in the tragedies of first one, then another World War as an almost halcyon period. Many view the time as one exhibiting a kind of innocence lost for ever in 1914. Secondly, contemporary photographs indicate that in terms of dress and fashion it was a time of elegance with very distinctive styles of wear for both men and women.

By the l890s, New Filey had established a 'fashionable' reputation. The distinction between Old Filey and New Filey was still a very real one, the dividing line being roughly along Murray Street. By this time the building of the Crescent and adjacent streets was complete; the Crescent Gardens also were laid out and available for strolling in, particularly after Sunday morning service. Filey's reputation as a resort 'free from all vulgarity' with good hotels, boarding houses and entertainment had become well established, and for a town of Filey's size the variety of shops was quite impressive.

16. The informal church parade after Sunday morning service about 1905.

17. The South Crescent Gardens about 1905.

One development that became apparent as Filey entered the 20th century was the wider range of leisure activities that residents and visitors found available in the town. Music was the basis for many forms of entertainment provided by both amateur and professional performers and, on occasion, those associated with the London stage could be seen and heard in Filey. In July 1901 booked to appear at the Victoria Hall, were Miss Irene Moncrieff, Miss Edith Broad, Mr. Llewelyn Cadwaladr and Mr. H. Carr-Evans, described as being from the Gaiety and Savoy Theatres, the D'Oyly Carte and Sir Augustus Harris Opera Companies. The Crescent Gardens Subscription Band was a very popular provider of light music during the season, usually playing both in the morning and evening.

The opening of the Grand Theatre on February 15th 1911 added a most important venue for a wide range of events. Not only was it designed to be both picture house and theatre, but it also had a tea room below the main entrance and a room suitable to be used either as a lecture or billiard room

In August 1913 two special occasions were the performance of *The Quaker Girl* by Mr George Dance's Company from the Adelphi Theatre, London, and from Daly's Theatre, Mr George Edwardes' Company in *The Merry Widow*. Rather less professional perhaps were the two Italian organ grinders who in September 1900 were fined 12 shillings each for continuing to play after being asked to desist. Seen also at the Grand in its earliest days were amateur productions such as *Pearl, The Fishermaiden,* one of many productions given by the Filey Amateur Operatic Society.

The Visitors' Lists indicate how holiday patterns were changing as the Victorian era gave way to the Edwardian. To 19th century Filey came men and women for a change of scene, health-giving sea air, gentle exercise and a little socialising; in many cases their children remained at home. However, by the early years of the 20th century the lists indicate that more children were now coming with their parents to the sea-side accompanied by maids, nurses and governesses. Filey was now seen to be a resort for all the family.

By Edwardian times in Filey there was a greater variety of amusements and entertainments than ever before. In addition to the orchestra which played in the Crescent Gardens, the Pierrots performed on the beach or Foreshore, the Golf Club was well established and there were opportunities for both residents and visitors to take part in Sports Days, Walking Matches or Hockey, Cricket and Football Matches. In 1906 a heated swimming pool, 60 feet by 19 feet, was built at Primrose Valley, primarily for the pupils of Southcliffe School, but also available to others. There were also the Liberal and Conservative Clubs, a Gymnastic and Athletic Club, a Cycling Club, and a Choral Society; University Extension Lectures and occasional Fancy Dress Balls. Between 1910 and 1912 there were also the daring young men in their flying machines performing astonishing aerial deeds from their base at Primrose Valley.

18. An earlier bandstand in the North Crescent Garden about 1910.

19. Unfortunately, the identity of this Edwardian days Crescent Gardens band is not known.

20. The Nansen Café stood on the Brigg where the Ornithological Group now has its hide.

21. A tree-lined Station Avenue as seen in Edwardian days.

The seemingly calm days we now think of as 'Edwardian' carried on after the death of King Edward VII in May 1910, and apparently even the weather of the period was good with long settled warm sunny spells. However, only a few short years remained before Europe was to be plunged into a cataclysm of violence from which few emerged unscathed.

Early Flying Days

The splendid beach of Filey Bay has been a significant factor in the development of Filey both as a fishing community and as a holiday resort. The use to which it was put in the early part of the 20th Century could not have been foreseen even a few years earlier.

The rapid development of powered flying machines can be said to have begun in December 1903 when Orville Wright achieved a flight of 40 yards. In October 1908, the American, Samuel Cody, made the first flight in Britain over a distance of nearly 500 yards. The early flying machines which soon followed this exploit generated great interest and enthusiasm and the Yorkshire Light Aeroplane Club was formed less than a year later. The necessity of a smooth surface for taking off and landing was of course immediately apparent to the first intrepid flyers and by the summer of 1910 the beach in Filey Bay was found to be just such a surface and for a time became Yorkshire's main take-off and landing strip.

The first positive step was the letter written by J. W. F. Tranmer on 2nd May 1910 to Filey Urban District Council requesting permission for himself 'and other aviators to carry out experiments with aeroplanes on Filey Sands'. Permission was granted by the Council members at their meeting the following day.

One of the first aircraft to arrive at Filey was a 25 h.p. Bleriot piloted by John William House of Bradford who in July 1910 combined his flying exploits with his honeymoon. His bride must have wondered if she had made a wise choice when soon after their arrival at Filey she saw his monoplane cartwheel on landing. Fortunately he emerged uninjured from the crash.

During the next two years Filonians followed with great interest the careers of the pilots and mechanics who came with their strange-looking aircraft. Within months a substantial hangar had been built on the Flat-Cliffs between Primrose Valley and Hunmanby Gap together with a concrete ramp to the beach. Remains of the ramp can still be seen on the cliff edge and an indication of the rate of coastal erosion can be obtained by imagining where the ramp would have originally reached the sand.

The hangar was used to house and service the aircraft brought by rail to Filey, and when it was no longer used for aircraft it was taken down and re-erected near Hunmanby Railway Station. Until relatively recently older

Filonians would refer to that part of the Flat Cliffs as 'near the hangar'. A bungalow was built for the aviators and ground crew.

Filey became the testing ground for the aircraft company formed by Robert Blackburn; the Blackburn Aircraft Company becoming one of the most successful aircraft companies with a world-wide reputation.

Robert Blackburn was born in Leeds in 1885 and qualified in engineering before working in a local ironworks managed by his father. Developing an interest in aircraft design, one of his early creations was described as a 'winged four-poster bed'. Another model piloted by Bentfield C. Hucks was used on the beach by the Filey Flying School.

B.C. Hucks, who had only just previously taught himself to fly here, was acknowledged to be the first English flyer to loop the loop, a manoeuvre which was then both difficult and dangerous; a press report in July 1914 described a loop he completed near Filey Railway Station roof. In May 1911 he became the first man to fly over Scarborough; the aircraft he used was the Blackburn Mercury with a 50 h.p. engine capable of a speed of 50 mph. The following day he crashed as a result of losing his propeller, though this was not serious for either plane or pilot although he lost consciousness while being carried to his lodgings.

The activities of the fliers were seriously marred on 6th December 1911 when a later Mercury model crashed, killing both the pilot, Hubert Oxley, and his passenger, Robert Weiss.

Another noted pilot who flew at Filey was John Brereton. A flight he made in May 1912 round the Bay so delighted the many spectators that he was 'heartily cheered' as he came in to land on the sands.

A less happy event took place in August 1911 when an aeroplane flew into Miss E.C. Pimlott of Hipperholme while she was on the beach. During Miss Pimlott's claim for damages at Leeds Town Hall she was represented by Mr. A.W. Bairstow, K.C., who described how she was swept into the air on a wing of the aeroplane and then thrown against the cliff. The jury awarded her £175 for her injuries which could well have been much more serious. The action was against Mr. Rupert Isaacson, a brilliant designer of engines who played a major part in building some of the first English aircraft. Frederick Handley Page and A.V.Roe, the founder of the Avro Aircraft Company, were two of the aviation pioneers who incorporated his engines in their aeroplanes.

In March, 1912, Robert Blackburn wrote from Balm Road, Leeds, to Filey Urban District Council to point out the expense the aviators were incurring by maintaining an aviation centre at Filey and to confirm that they would have to move elsewhere if no financial support was made available to them. The aviators were keen to remain in Filey Bay as they wished to develop a hydroplane; however the members of the Council did not feel able to offer any financial assistance and so the short, but intensely interesting chapter of Filey's involvement in the early history of flying closed.

In 1960 a jubilee celebration was arranged to commemorate the beginning of flying in Filey in 1910. The programme for 12th July gives the timetable of events including the landing on the beach of a 1932 Blackburn B.2 Trainer and six runs of a Blackburn Beverley over the Bay for parachutists to drop into the water, some with inflatable craft and some to be picked up by R.A.F. launch.

The Motor Car Comes To Filey

The closing years of the 19th Century saw the rapid development of the horseless carriage and the introduction of motor transport by which everyday life was to be so dramatically changed. Daimler patented his first light high-speed engine in 1883 and Benz is credited with making his first tricycle in 1885. Henry Ford built his first car in 1896. The earliest British car was perhaps the Lanchester-built vehicle in 1895. Subsequently development was very rapid indeed and in 1900 the Automobile Club of Great Britain organised a 1000 mile Trial around England and Wales. By 1896 the maximum speed limit for a mechanically-propelled vehicle was raised to 12 mph and it no longer became necessary for the vehicle to be preceded by a man on foot.

Though Filey was not on a main through road there were several occasions during those early motoring days when the sound of the internal combustion engine was heard in the streets and on the beach. A particularly exciting day was Whit Monday 1905 when the Yorkshire Automobile Club held inaugural speed trials over a distance of two miles on the beach. There had been previously some concern that the sand might not be firm enough to bear the weight of the vehicles and so at the request of the Automobile Club of Great Britain, Mr. H.R. Kirk of Leeds tested the beach in his Gordon-Bennet Winner and reached the remarkable speed of just under 80 mph on very wet sands.

The Yorkshire Automobile Club's headquarters for the occasion were the Royal Crescent Hotel where over one hundred members and friends were entertained to dinner on the first evening of the Meeting. Eight events were arranged for entries varying from the 6 hp de Dion of Mr. Alfred Masser of Leeds to the 90 hp Napier of Mr. Cecil Edge from London, and the course along the beach was marked out by a single-furrow plough drawn by two horses. Thousands of spectators arrived on the day to witness the trials. The highest speed was the 72 mph achieved by Mr. Edge's Napier; another impressive performance was the 62mph of Mr. Huntley Walker's 70 hp touring Darracq. An unanticipated problem for the organisers was due to the fact that the mass of spectators on the beach was such that the force exerted on the sand brought water to the surface making it necessary to change the course. The confusion this caused resulted in many onlookers leaving before the trials were completed. A remarkable day ended with the presentation of prizes by Mrs. Arthur Clay at the Crescent Hotel.

22. Motor trials, 12th June 1905.

The difficulties of driving on the beach were not always appreciated, as Mr. W.T. Lord of Wigan found to his cost. In April 1907 he had taken a party for a spin on the beach. All went well until they stopped near Primrose Valley to take photographs. On attempting to resume their jaunt, Mr. Lord found the car was sinking in the sand — and the tide was coming in. Fortunately, help was at hand in the shape of horses drawing fish carts, and an urgent request for assistance was made. The cartmen clearly saw an opportunity not to be missed and made a bargain by which the party was required to purchase the total load of fish before a rescue would be attempted. The visitors, now a little wiser, completed their jaunt by arranging the auction of their unexpectedly acquired catch.

A case heard at Filey Police Court in September 1906 is illustrative of the early days of motoring. It arose as a result of an incident in Scarborough Road when Lord and Lady Aukland had just set off, with their son, on a cycle ride to Scarborough. A motorist, Francis Sutcliffe of Halifax, overtook them at a 'distinctly dangerous pace — not less than 20 miles an hour' according to Lord Aukland, although Mr. Sutcliffe claimed he had slowed to 6 or 7 miles an hour. What was agreed was that heated words were exchanged particularly with regard to the Aukland's dog which, it was admitted, was walking 'on the wrong side of the road'. Although the defendant fainted twice during the case and was tended solicitously by her Ladyship, he did not elicit the bench's sympathy who found the charge of reckless driving proved and fined him 40s and costs.

Darkness held particular problems for early motorists. A party from London en route from Scarborough to Hull in August 1906 took a wrong turning and found themselves, after midnight, travelling down Queen Street unaware that it was a cul-de-sac. A bad accident was avoided at the last moment by 'prompt brake action alone'. The incident, not surprisingly, prompted a call for all night street lighting.

Filonians in the early years of the century gradually adjusted, like others, to the increasing number of vehicles on the streets and the replacement of horses by the internal combustion engine as a means of propulsion As in other resorts the problem of parking became apparent in later years and as a partial answer to this in the late 1930s a field in Station Avenue was converted to a car-park. During the Second World War it was used by the forces as a parade ground. In post-war years a bus station was established there; previously buses for Scarborough took passengers on board in Union Street outside Trinity Church and passengers for Bridlington waited in Station Avenue near the Corner Café.

As increasing numbers of vehicles appeared on Filey streets so did single and double yellow lines and one-way signs. The Station Avenue roundabout was one traffic feature about which opinions differed in the early 1960s. A small field at the junction of Station Avenue and Station Road was acquired in order to build the roundabout and the remaining portion of the field was used to create the present open garden and shelter.

Filey is fortunate that it has always had a by-pass and therefore its problems have never been added to by through traffic. The Plan for Filey of 1943 proposed a road from Royal Oak Crossing alongside the railway line and linked to West Avenue by a roundabout which would also be joined to the Crescent by a road crossing what is now Glen Gardens. Perhaps it is as well this plan never came to fruition!

World War One

The years preceding the Great War were unsettled ones during which a succession of crises in Central Europe had brought the realisation that there was a real possibility of war. The assassination of the Archduke Ferdinand in Sarajevo late in June 1914 precipitated a series of events which culminated in the armies of Germany moving towards France through neutral Belgium. This action resulted in Great Britain entering the conflict on August 4th in defence of Belgium and thus began the four-year struggle.

Even before the war was declared, many on holiday in Filey felt it advisable to return home early and numerous August and September bookings were cancelled. It soon became apparent that what had begun as a promising season was to be a very disappointing one. For boarding-house keepers, hoteliers and shopkeepers the financial implications were worrying.

The rush of volunteers to join the forces soon resulted in Filey becoming a garrison-town as troops were billeted in the now readily available and often commandeered accommodation. After an interval of one hundred years since the Napoleonic wars, defences against invasion were once again established and sand bags and barbed wire were much in evidence.

The fear of invasion was very real, a point starkly made within one month of the outbreak of war by the Chief Constable of the East Riding who warned that anyone who was observed to be showing a light near the cliffs was liable to be shot on sight. Some preparations for the repulsion of invasion forces had been made in the years prior to the outbreak of war; in the summer of 1912 regular and territorial army units totalling 15,000 men engaged in defensive manoeuvres in the Filey district.

Four months only were to elapse before the realities of war were brought home very dramatically to the local population. Early in the morning of December 16th a force of six German cruisers approached the coast off Whitby. The *Seydlitz, Moltke* and *Blücher* then steamed north towards the Tees and the *Derrflinger, Von Der Tann* and *Kolberg* headed south for Scarborough. Soon after 8.00 a.m. the *Derrflinger* and *Von Der Tann* appeared out of the mist to begin a bombardment of the town at a range of about one mile. In the raid nineteen people were killed, many were injured and considerable damage was caused by the several hundred shells which fell on the town. The damaged buildings included the Castle, the Grand and Royal Hotels, St. Martin's Church and Dunollie in Filey Road. The noise of the bombardment was clearly heard in Filey and many dressed hurriedly believing invasion to be imminent. By 8.30 a.m. the raid was over but a bitter harvest was still to be garnered for, while Scarborough was being bombarded, the *Kolberg* proceeded past Filey and Flamborough Head laying mines as she went. Perhaps the intention was that the mines would be a barrier to vessels of the English Fleet approaching from the south, but, in the event, fourteen merchant vessels, two trawlers and four minesweepers became victims with the loss of over one hundred lives.

Although the operational range of German aircraft was insufficient to enable them to reach Northern England, bombing raids by Zeppelins brought first-hand experience of war to civilians. Local defence against these raiders was provided by BE2c biplanes based on Scarborough Racecourse; one tactic consisted of attempting to fly over the Zeppelin so that grenades could be dropped on it.

Of the many troops who were billeted and trained in Filey, the ones most frequently recalled by residents in later years were the men of the Hunts Cyclists Battalion. Because of the length of time they were stationed here it was said of them that the War Office had forgotten them. Whatever the reason, many friendships were established between residents and soldiers and several marriages also resulted. Consequently some men settled in Filey after the war and in the vicinity of Huntingdon there are families with antecedents from the Filey area. The Border Regiment was another unit which established long lasting links with Filey. Not surprisingly, Filey was chosen as a suitable town in which those wounded in battle could convalesce, and Osborne House, staffed by V. A. D. nurses, was one of the houses adapted for this purpose.

The residents made the best of difficult times. For four years the town's income from visitors was minimal and there was little paid war work in the neighbourhood. Rationing was introduced, adding to the general hardship, and worst of all, all too frequently, the local paper reported Filey men who had been wounded or killed in action. So often they were young, sometimes barely out of their teens. During the course of the war many awards for gallantry were made to local men.

One of the most difficult times of the whole conflict was in 1917 when severe reverses were experienced on land, and at sea the German U-boat offensive was so effective that England was considered by many to be in real danger of starvation. The shortage of food was such that imprisonment could be the result of a conviction for wasting bread.

Of all U K shipping lanes, one of the most dangerous was that between the Humber and the Tees with the waters off Flamborough Head being a notoriously hazardous area. Several vessels were sunk close to Filey, usually by torpedo, and many lives were lost. Some of these tragedies took place so close to the coast that they were clearly witnessed by farmworkers from the cliff top. Amongst the vessels torpedoed in waters close to Filey Brigg were the *Ardens* of

1300 tonnes, the *Norhilda,* 1200 tonnes, both in August 1917, the *Ballogie* of 1200 tonnes and the *Isabelle* of 2,500 tonnes in November 1917. More than 20 seamen perished in the loss of these ships.

In the days before radar it was relatively safe for submarines to surface after nightfall. In July 1917 one U-boat made an emergency dive while two sailors were still on deck. They were however sufficiently close in to swim ashore and were captured by a military patrol near Cloughton.

A factor in overcoming the U-boat menace was the introduction of the convoy system. The lateness of its development is surprising in view of the fact that it had proved so effective in several earlier times of war from the days of Oliver Cromwell onwards.

On the mainland of Europe battles raged with undiminished fury into 1918 when the German Spring Offensive dealt a devastating blow to the Allied Forces. However, subsequent developments favoured the Allied cause and peace finally returned to an exhausted land in November.

In Filey, soldiers and sailors returned to resume their civilian lives, but there were many local families for whom cherished members would never return; when the entrance to the Memorial Gardens was built 73 names were inscribed on its Roll of Honour.

The first post-war peacetime year, 1919, was separated from the previous peacetime year, 1913, by only six years, but to many it must have seemed an eternity in time, for so much had taken place and so many lives had been changed in the interim.

Between the Wars

The First World War drew wearily to a close in November 1918. In Filey as throughout Britain there was less a feeling of elation than a sense of relief that at last it was all over, even though the conclusion was an Armistice rather than complete victory. There was also in the town a permeating sadness that many who had joined the army or the navy with a real sense of duty, would not return.

In its appearance Filey had experienced little change. Almost no new building had taken place during the war years and many properties witnessed to the minimal amount of maintenance that had been carried out since 1914. The town centre was also scarred by the remains of two major buildings recently destroyed by fire; Trinity Methodist Church burnt down in January 1918 and the Victoria Hall in Murray Street about the same time. In neither case was the cause of the fire ever satisfactorily established. The church was rebuilt on the same site and the hall was eventually replaced by shops.

The years following the war were difficult ones; the national economy recovered only slowly and it was soon evident that visitors were not returning in hoped-for numbers. Fishermen returning from mine-sweeping duties found a

23. Thomas Marr was one of several Filey butchers.

24. The Royal Filey Pierrots on the beach about 1920.

25. This race meeting took place on the 15th September 1923; the 1½ mile race was for the Filey Tradesmen's Cup.

26. Shortly before World War II, holiday-makers enjoy a day on the beach.

rapidly changing industry. Yawls were no more to be seen fishing on the Yorkshire coast and powered vessels were now in greater use. The early post-war years were very good for North Sea fishing as stocks had been able to recover with the reduction in numbers of deep-sea trawlers.

Filey in the 1920s was not as hard hit by high levels of unemployment as were many industrial towns; fish was still caught and sold and people continued to come on holiday. There was however a shortage of jobs and several local men, on the recommendation of a visiting clergyman, moved with their families to take work at the Staveley Ironworks near Chesterfield.

The wireless was an increasingly popular source of entertainment and householders with no mains electricity took batteries to Abbott's shop on West Avenue to be recharged.

Alternative means of travel to the London and North Eastern Railway were provided by Scarborough District Motors who provided a service from the Post Office in Murray Street, and by the Blue Bus Service, which had a 'fleet of Modern Pneumatic-Tyred Saloon Buses'. The increasing number of motorists was provided for by Parker's Central Garage near the Crescent and Taylor's Station Garage. For those who journeyed further afield by train, fares changed little between the wars and in 1939 a return ticket to London cost just 8d more than £2.00.

In the Post World War I days the British Legion soon became the important ex-Service organisation it remains today. Premises were acquired at 22 Brooklands (now the Youth Centre), and opened as the British Legion and United Services Club.

Another much appreciated facility was the library which opened in West Avenue in 1933 as one of the first purpose-built libraries in the East Riding.

To cater for the increasing expectations of residents and visitors, the Southdene Pavilion opened as a dance-hall in 1925 and several years later was equipped with a stage so that it could be used as a theatre. The spirit of the '30s is evoked by the names of the concert parties engaged for the summer season of 1937; Holiday Fair, Royal Quixotes, Gala Revels, Swingtime, Kit-Kat Kits, Smile a While, Vivacity, Crazy Follies, Summertime Cabaret, and Live Wires; each party entertained for one week.

Two unwelcome events of the 1930s were first an earth tremor early in the decade which caused the upper section of Trinity Church steeple to twist out of line, and a 'flu epidemic in April 1937 which affected one third of the town's inhabitants and caused all the schools to be closed for one month.

The inter-war years saw limited developments taking place at Primrose Valley. This small vale, appropriately named in its earlier days, was initially popular for simple camping but the advent of the family motor-car brought more visitors and also some permanent residents to this previously quiet part of the Bay.

27. The Ravine Hall in use as an hotel in the 1930s. The Glen Gardens Café now stands there.

28. For many on holiday in the 1930s (and later) it was essential to hire a beach tent.

29. Cargate Hill and Kingston Cottage about 1930.

The middle years of the 1930s saw the national economy strengthening and this resulted in more prosperous times for Filey and in particular its hotels, boarding-houses and shops. However, just when it seemed that Filey could reasonably look forward to a happier time, events in Germany were beginning to cast a shadow over the whole of Europe.

World War Two

The year preceding the outbreak of the Second World War in September 1939 had been for Filey, as for the rest of the country, a period of tension and uncertainty. Since Mr. Chamberlain's return from his meeting at Munich with Herr Hitler the likelihood of war had become increasingly apparent and preparations for that eventuality were being made.

When finally war was declared on September 3rd events in Filey began to happen quite quickly. The previous day a Food Control Committee was formed and the contracts for The Majors (the Crescent Gardens Orchestra) and the Red Admirals (the Southdene Concert Party) were terminated with some financial compensation. Sand-bags for vulnerable buildings were filled in large numbers on the beach and Ben Hindle, Clerk to Filey Urban District Council, was appointed both Local Fuel Overseer and Food Executive Officer. Evacuees soon began to arrive from Hull and Hartlepool and were billeted with local families who received about 8 shillings (40p) per week for each child. The organisers were able to report that 1312 evacuees, almost all children and mothers, had been billeted in the Filey area, a quite remarkable achievement. The considerable increase in Filey's school age population meant that for the first few weeks half-time schooling was instituted with local children and evacuees alternating mornings and afternoons on a weekly basis.

A First-Aid Post was built on to the Station Avenue side of Trinity Methodist Church Schoolroom, occupying a section of the footpath and part of the road. The lighter shade of the stonework of the church is still discernible. Presumably the stones were scrubbed as they had become an interior wall.

On October 3rd, the Military requisitioned the Southdene Pavilion and adjacent tennis courts and very many other local premises were taken over by the forces. Number 11, The Beach, known then and now as 'The Anchorage' became a Sick Bay for evacuees and continued so for a long period even though by November 7th it was reported that 655, almost exactly half, of the evacuees had returned home. The anticipated air-raids on major cities had not taken place and evacuees continued to return home, though some remained for the duration of the war. West Vale, built shortly before the war as an estate of bungalows for holiday letting, was commandeered for the use of evacuee families.

As the number of men and women called up increased, so forces stationed in and around Filey grew in strength and as winter approached, dark, off-duty evenings were not easy to fill. In November, the Officer Commanding

125th Officer Cadet Training Unit, Royal Artillery, asked for the Filey cinemas to be allowed to open on Sunday evenings; this request elicited the reply from the licensing authorities that further enquiries would have to be made.

The threat of raids by enemy bombers had been anticipated before the outbreak of war and in January 1939 a system of Air Raid Precautions (A.R.P.) was set up with eleven Sector Warden Posts. This was reduced in January 1940 to four Sector Posts. The Wardens had a social club situated over the Gas Showrooms and on the roof of the same building was placed the siren which gave notice of an air raid with a sound of varying frequency, and of the 'all clear' with a steady note.

Sea mines laid in the busy East Coast shipping lane were a menace which led to the loss of many ships on the Yorkshire coast. Occasionally, mines would break loose from their moorings and float to explode on impact with rock, cliff or beach. One such incident resulted in the destruction of the café on the Brigg. In order to prevent, if possible, risk to life or damage to property, Filey Urban District Council, in March 1940, offered via the Filey Fishermen's Society, the sum of £5 to any fisherman who would tow away a threatening, floating mine. No suggestions were made as to where they might take it. On occasion, a mine observed floating in the Bay would result in the evacuation of Foreshore Road residents.

Nothing in the Filey district caused it to be considered as a strategic area; however, on several occasions incendiary and high explosive bombs were dropped on Filey. During the night of 19th-20th August 1940 two H.E. bombs were dropped in the West Avenue area. One fell in the garden of Tile Cottage demolishing the greenhouse and causing damage to many houses in the neighbourhood. A collection for the W.V.S. was soon organised from those who went to view the crater. Several more fell around Filey in following nights. The biggest conflagration was caused just before 9 pm on 25th February 1941 when considerable fire damage resulted from bombs falling on the laundry in Laundry Road. These and other raids on the town emphasised the importance of maintaining an effective black-out and a well-organised A.R.P. team ensured that there were no lights visible to enemy aircraft passing overhead. Many aircraft, both of the Allied and enemy air forces crashed in the area during the war years.

A Vickers Wellington crash-landed in fields (where is now Filey School) in August 1940 after running out of fuel following a raid on Hamburg; all members of the crew were uninjured. The aircraft was subsequently repaired and returned to service.

For use in air raids, available to householders, were Anderson Shelters which were erected in gardens partly below ground level and with a roof of corrugated iron and heaped-up earth. The Morrison Shelter was for indoor use and consisted of a flat iron sheet resting on corner iron supports. Before erecting the shelter it was necessary to strengthen the floor. As Filey was on the coast the air raid warning siren was frequently in use and residents spent many hours in shelters, under staircases or at front doors discussing which way the bombers were going.

In addition to sea mines and bombs, there was a hazard for the unwary in the land-mines that were laid in the cliffs around the Bay in case of invasion. These were a danger for many years in spite of warning notices, particularly as in time much cliff slippage took place. Arndale was one area local residents knew to avoid.

In 1940, after the fall of Dunkirk, it was known that preparations were being made for the invasion of Britain. The possibility that this would take place as far north as the Yorkshire coast was taken seriously and many preventative measures were taken. Residents concealed their most prized possessions beneath floor boards and received instructions on what to do in case of invasion. Road blocks were erected at strategic points, a concrete block-house occupied almost all the space under the Promenade bridge and other approaches to the beach were also blocked. The vantage point in the Glen Gardens which provides a clear sea view is in fact the roof of a block-house which at war's end was earthed up as an alternative to demolition. On the Coble Landing a narrow access was left for the lifeboat and cobles. On the beach itself lines of concrete blocks were erected at right angles to the cliff and Promenade and iron posts were sunk into the sand and clay beneath, to prevent troop-carrying aircraft or gliders from landing. For a time the coastal region was declared a prohibited area for casual visitors and a night-time curfew was enforced.

After 1941 the threat of invasion diminished as the war progressed and tension in Filey eased; however, Filey Bay still contains, particularly in the vicinity of Reighton Gap, many structures erected in the early days of the war.

Although with time there was less need for anti-invasion forces to be stationed in the district, Filey remained for the duration a training area. A premium was, of course, placed on physical fitness and small areas were developed for agility training and as they consisted mainly of ropes suspended from tall trees they were a joy for and a challenge to local youth. Three areas so festooned were, the trees forming the boundary between the South Crescent putting green and Glen Gardens, the trees behind Downcliffe, and the upper part of Church Ravine which is now Church Cliff Drive.

The Royal Crescent Hotel was one of many hotels taken over by the forces and on occasion the local Officer Commanding would take the salute from the balcony over the main entrance for the march-past after Sunday morning church parade.

During the war the tradition of going away on holiday was discouraged; the railway stations carried posters asking 'Is Your Journey Really Necessary?' and 'Holiday At Home' weeks were organised for inland towns. There would have been little purpose in a visitor coming to Filey; access to the beach was denied or only allowed for a small part; the golf course was an army training ground and most boarding houses and hotels were occupied by evacuees or forces personnel.

Architecturally unprepossessing, but necessary to wartime Filey, were the static water tanks for fire engines erected in case water mains were broken in an air raid. The tanks were circular in shape with walls about 5 feet in height. One stood in the Crescent Gardens in front of the Royal Crescent Hotel, another was erected on the Foreshore where the paddling pool now is.

The many groups of service personnel who were stationed in Filey included for a time a large contingent of the Free French Air Force whose members were well received by local people and many lasting friendships were established.

In spite of food rationing, black-out, curfew and other inconveniences as well as the considerable fall in the town's overall income, the life of the community carried on. Those not called to the forces took on extra responsibilities in the Home Guard, as Special Constables or A.R.P. Wardens; the Churches, the W.V.S. and Y.M.C.A. established canteens for the forces. The unavailability of petrol for private motoring was not a major problem as relatively few local residents had cars. Those who were able were encouraged to 'Dig For Victory' and take an allotment or change lawns into vegetable patches. Filey had three allotment areas; Muston Road, Scarborough Road and close to the Golf Club approach road now grassed over and used as a seasonal car park.

After almost six years of war, peace returned. V.E. (Victory in Europe) Day was celebrated in May 1945 in Filey with dancing in Murray Street, an unusual and for those taking part, a slightly self-conscious activity. Three months later the war in the Far East was over and Britain began to face the many problems of peacetime.

In Filey, families and friends continued to mourn the 52 local men who had given their lives during the conflict.

The Post-War Years,

In 1945, Filey moved from war to peace-time in reasonable shape by comparison with many other similar sized communities. The relatively small amount of bomb damage had been made good and much of the anti-invasion work had been removed. Although the forces occupying the hotels and boarding-houses for much of the war had not been the most considerate of tenants, compensation for damage was paid by the War Department, if not always as generously as owners thought appropriate. The war in Europe ended in May and hostilities in the Far East in early August, so Filey did enjoy something of a summer season. Many, for whom six long years had passed since their most recent proper summer holiday, took the opportunity to return to the seaside. They found the beach still adorned with several lines of concrete blocks, tall iron posts and tubular steel frameworks although the metal was now much corroded and many of the concrete blocks had crumbled. However, the concrete block-houses situated on the cliffs around the bay were still in quite good condition although some were in the process of sliding down the eroded cliffs.

Rationing of provisions was still to be a fact of life for several peace-time years as was conscription for the forces, but Filey soon resumed a peace-time appearance with few uniforms in evidence. The streets by present-day standards were quiet with relatively few cars to be seen even during the season. Most journeys in or out of town were made by bus or train and the service bus route was via Mitford Street, Union Street and Station Avenue with the stop for Scarborough positioned in Union Street outside Trinity Church entrance, and passengers for Bridlington and Hunmanby waited in Station Avenue close to the Corner Café.

The ending of the 'black-out' and the resumption of street lighting by gas-lamps removed the hazards of after-dark journeys on foot through the town; provided such outings were completed by midnight when most lamps were extinguished.

Filey in the late 1940s had a range of shops rather different from that which is available now. The number of butchers' shops has barely changed, but in pre-supermarket days there were several grocers and provision-merchants as well as more tailors, outfitters and furniture dealers.

In 1946 the perhaps strange decision was made to move the fire-station to the newly opened Butlin's Camp; however, in 1950 it moved to its present site in Mitford Street.

The first television sets were in use in Filey in 1951-52, but it was several years before T.V. became a significant leisure activity. The first signal was a black and white B.B.C. channel followed by a poor definition I.T.V. programme. In spite of very considerable changes in the value of money the price of a small black and white T.V. at about £60 has hardly changed since; a tribute, no doubt, to a continuous process of improving technology.

Not a resident, but someone who entered for a while into the life of Filey, was Richard Hoggart, author of the influential Penguin book 'The Uses of Literacy' and later, Assistant Director-General of U.N.E.S.C.O. In 1949, while on the staff of Hull University Department of Adult Education, he was responsible for a series of 24 lectures on 'The Modern Novel'. These were given at the Cosy Café in Hope Street. The fee for the course was 5/6d (28p).

The two cinemas were very important providers of entertainment with frequent, comfortably full houses, particularly on Saturday evenings. Cinemagoers then expected a balanced programme of 'shorts', trailers for coming films, a newsreel and a main feature, and finally the National Anthem.

A welcome sign of return to normality was the engagement of a small orchestra to play in the bandstand in the Crescent Gardens. The oval stand was in place in front of the balcony.

30. The Crescent Gardens in the mid-1950s.

31. Martin's barrier was built by Edwin Martin to protect his
Ravine Hall estate. It was severely damaged in the storm of January, 1953.

32. Built in 1904, Deepdene was a family home on the sea-front until the 1960s.

In 1949 notice was given to the Filey Urban District Council to leave their premises in West Avenue and so a move was made to the Cottage, a large house overlooking the sea just south of Foords Hotel. The Council remained here until moving to the building which is now the Evron Centre.

One of the worst storms of the century occurred at the end of January 1953; it resulted in extremely high tides, very severe flooding, and considerable loss of life in England and Holland. In Filey, the Foreshore Road was submerged and the wooden barriers, south of Crescent Hill, were damaged beyond repair. Plans were soon drawn up for a more substantial replacement and in July 1955 the newly completed Royal Parade was opened by the Princess Royal.

The Southdene Pavilion was for many post-war years a valued entertainment facility with Variety Shows and a Repertory Company in the summer. During several years the variety and drama companies alternated between the Southdene Pavilion and Butlin's Camp. In the winter the Church Youth Club Pantomime produced by Frank Scaife to an always high standard was an eagerly awaited event.

The particular needs of older members of the community were recognised in January 1962 with the opening of the Elderly Persons' Club in what had been a fisherman's cottage at 19 Queen Street, and a donation of £500 from W E Butlin enabled the club to be comfortably furnished. The club was not however to remain there long as later in the year the decision was made, to the regret of many, to demolish the cottages, and Providence Place (known to many as 'Jenk Alley') was chosen for a new development of flats and a club for the elderly.

A change in leisure activities was indicated by the reduction in demand for allotment gardens. In pre-war and war-time days allotments were available off Muston Road and Scarborough Road and close to the road to the Golf Club, but now the Muston Road site was found to be sufficient The West Avenue site became a field available as an overflow car park and the Scarborough Road land was sold for private house building. The proceeds from this sale were retained by the Town Council and the interest from its investment used for maintaining facilities in the town and allocating grants to voluntary bodies. An issue which, at the time, generated considerable feeling in the town, was the proposal by Filey Urban District Council in 1970 to create a Country Park from agricultural land north of St. Oswald's Church. Many believed it was an undesirable development and mounted a vigorous campaign against it; however, the plans were carried through with most of the opposers later reaching the opinion that their fears had been groundless.

Changing holiday patterns resulted in many boarding-houses and hotels being converted to flats for letting or sale and as Filey entered the 1980s a further change, reflecting a national trend, saw conversions to homes for the elderly.

The re-organisation of local government in 1974 had two major effects on Filey; the County boundaries were redrawn placing Filey, previously in the East Riding, in North Yorkshire and the town becoming part of the Borough of Scarborough. Filey's Urban District Council was reformed as a Town Council with fewer powers but with, for the first time, the right to appoint a Mayor.

Changes in holiday patterns, leisure activities and retail shopping affected Filey as it did other similarly sized resorts. The conversion through the 1960s and 1970s of hotels and boarding houses to flats reduced the numbers of holiday-makers staying in the town. Another factor contributing to the same change was the growth in size of and facilities offered by holiday villages between Reighton Gap and Cayton Bay. Filey beach and shops attract holiday-makers from these 'villages' during the day, thus giving the town and sea-front a busy appearance, but summer evenings are quieter as visitors return to chalets, caravans and entertainment complexes. Television has also led to a reduction in the popularity of traditional sea-side variety shows, and the Brig Cinema met the fall in numbers of filmgoers by introducing live entertainment and then converting a major part of the building to a shopping centre. This conversion followed the adjacent green-field development of a supermarket and arcade of shops.

A new venture began in 1970 when it was suggested by Filey U.D.C., to the newly-formed Local History Society, that two cottages in Queen Street, scheduled for demolition, might in fact be opened by the society as a Museum. On acceptance of this suggestion the property was renovated by the Council and rewired and redecorated by the local Lions Club. After the premises were opened officially by Miss Lucy Owston of Hunmanby in May 1971, seven rooms of exhibits were available to visitors at admission charges, for the first few seasons, of 5p and 2½p.

From Filey's uncertain origins as a small and spartan settlement, a span of perhaps thirteen centuries has brought it to an age when its inhabitants can communicate across the globe, stay warm and well fed through the hardest winter, fly to distant lands for holidays in the sun, and have leisure time to do things out of interest rather than from necessity. How the early Filonians (and many of later years) would have marvelled at such opportunities.

CHAPTER FIVE

The Town

Buildings

For most of its history the domestic part of Filey consisted almost entirely of what is now Queen Street together with adjoining groups of dwellings.

The community was, for several centuries, a fishing and farming village of a few hundred inhabitants. Only for a relatively short period in the 16th and 17th centuries apparently did Filey have a manor house of its own; this was the home of the Buck(e) family and was situated immediately to the north of the Parish Church. Some earthworks are still visible, though nothing of the building now remains above ground; presumably when occupation ceased the materials were removed for use elsewhere

The oldest domestic building is that now occupied by Filey Museum at 8-10 Queen Street. The plaque above the door of number 8 has inscribed on it the year 1696 and it would seem likely the plaque was placed there on construction or later alteration of what was a fairly substantial cottage. Church Hill has some 18th century houses including one with a plaque indicating a date of 1716.

The expansion of Filey began with the building of several 'villas'. These were detached properties erected in fringe areas of *Old* Filey and included Grove Villa (now replaced by a modern building) in Scarborough Road, North Cliff Villa (replaced by a later North Cliff), and South Cliff Villas (immediately to the south of Cargate Hill). One of the very earliest buildings erected with visitors in mind was a bath house situated at the junction of Murray Street and West Avenue where is now a chemist's shop.

The then most distant property from *Old* Filey was Ravine Villa (later Ravine Hall), a Georgian style building situated in its own grounds which now comprise the Glen Gardens. It was built by Henry Bentley of Bentley's Yorkshire Beers in 1837-38 and the ravine which marked the southern boundary of this small estate thus became known as Bentley's Gill. The present name of Martin's Ravine came into use in 1889 when Edwin Martin, a Huddersfield mill owner, purchased the property. The lodge in West Avenue and carriage drive still remain almost unaltered. Filey is fortunate that the grounds were eventually brought into public ownership. Ravine Hall was demolished in the 1970s and replaced by the Glen Gardens Café.

33. Belle Vue Street and the Royal Hotel, about 1885.

One of the earliest New Filey properties was Cliff House (now the Bronte Café) in Belle Vue Street; built about 1842 it was to enjoy an uninterrupted sea-view for only a few years. Across the road, but erected about 20 years later, is the Belle Vue, one of Filey's very few purpose built hotels. An hotel that was apparently planned, but never built, was the Prince of Wales; proposed in August 1899, the chosen site was Station Avenue. An ambitious scheme which also never came to fruition was announced in August 1894. If it had been successfully completed there would have been a sea-wall and promenade to the Brigg and, where is now the Country Park, a large estate of domestic buildings with public gardens and fountains at street intersections. A pier, 600 yards in length, was also planned and the total estimated cost was one million pounds.

One of the most satisfying domestic buildings is Church Cliff House immediately to the north-west of St. Oswald's Church; of late 18th or early 19th century construction, it has a splendid Georgian style door, six bays on the east front and five on the south front. The adjacent square stone dovecot is an unusual and fine feature.

By far the greatest influence in the development of New Filey was that of John Wilkes Unett, a Birmingham solicitor, born in 1770 and co-founder of the Birmingham Society of Arts. When he first came to Filey is not known, but

34. Fishermen's cottages in Queen Street; to the regret of many, they were demolished in the mid 1960s.

35. Queen Street today.

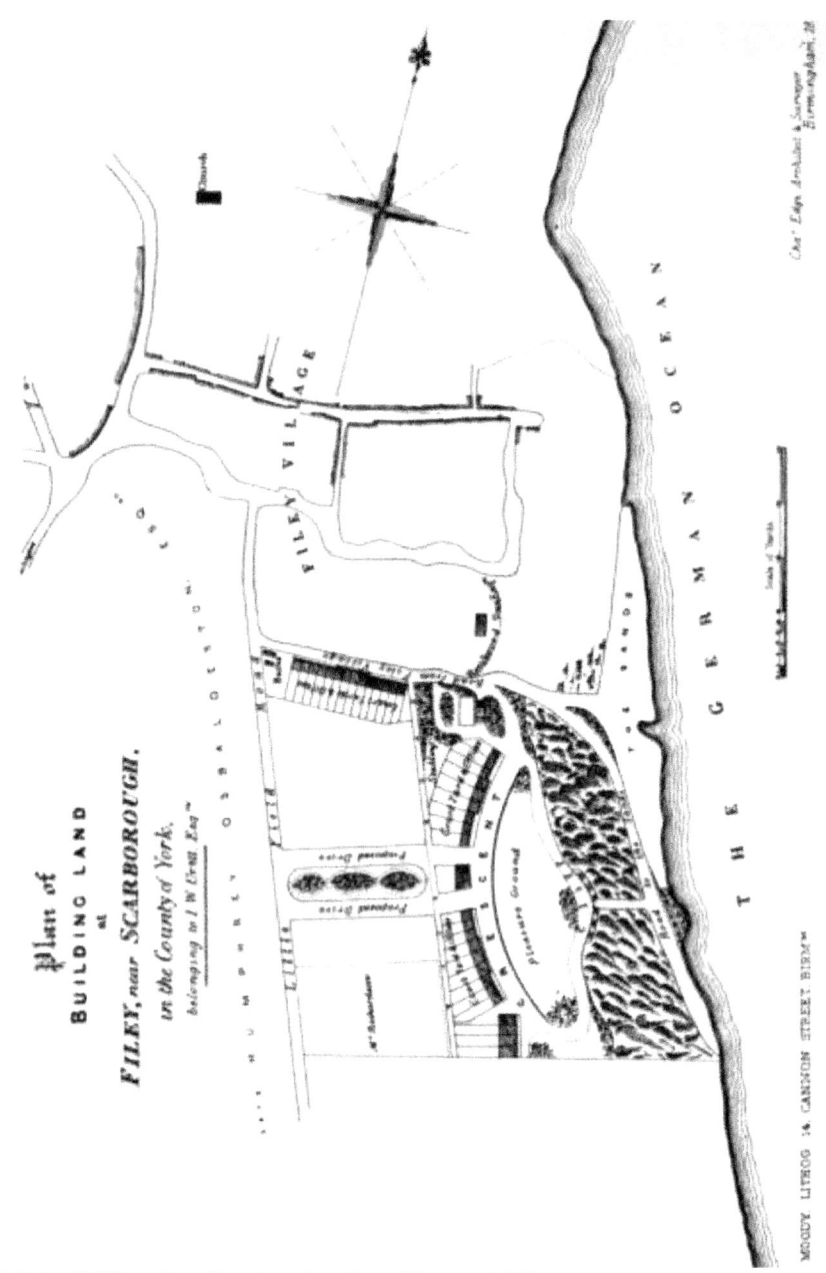

36. John Wilkes Unett's plan for New Filey in 1835.

by 1835 he had purchased several acres of land and had caused to be drawn up plans for what was to become New Filey. These plans indicate that properties similar to those on the Crescent were proposed for what is now Murray Street. Clearly he was a man of vision and determined that the development should be worthy of the site and the result was, in part, the Crescent; a group of domestic buildings which can be claimed to be one of the finest in the North of England. To include in the design, pleasure gardens for the full length of the Crescent, was an idea for which residents and visitors have been profoundly grateful now for a century and a half. The first block to be built was that between Rutland Street and Brooklands (numbers 8-14) and was completed in the 1840s. This small terrace has Greek Doric porches and a continuous cast iron balcony at first floor level. The second block to be built (numbers 1-7) soon followed in 1851. The end elevations are particularly impressive with Corinthian pilasters and a pediment. The centre piece of the whole design, the Crescent Hotel, was completed in 1853. One feature of this building is the Venetian window over the central porch, another is the cast iron balcony at first floor level. The hotel was considerably enlarged on the western side later in the century and it is not difficult to see from the difference in styles where the two parts join together. The remainder of the Crescent was erected in subsequent years with number 38 (Osborne House) carrying the date 1890.

Except for the hotel, all the Crescent properties were houses intended for residence or for boarding, but in time the functions of many changed as two or more were amalgamated to form hotels. As a result several lost their separate entrances as doors were converted to windows. An interesting exercise is to identify the original entrances from number 15 onwards.

Of the same period as the early Crescent houses, but of rather different style, is Rutland Terrace, now numbers 24-38 Rutland Street. Built in 1847 these houses have full height, bow-fronted bay windows and together form a satisfying group. Contemporaneous with Rutland Terrace but much different in appearance was Clarence Place (27-41 West Avenue) still known to many for obvious reasons as Red Brick Row. Building continued behind the Crescent up to and after the turn of the century. West Avenue is so named because it formed the western boundary of Unett's estate with Belle Vue Street, Rutland Street and Brooklands, being originally named North Street, Middle Street and South Street, and Southdene previously being known as Unett Street. John Street still retains the name given to it to commemorate the estate developer.

Another detached domestic building of note was South Crescent Villa built about 1850; considerably and sympathetically enlarged, it is now the White Lodge Hotel. The first building to be erected immediately to the south of Cargate Hill was known as 1 and 2 South Cliff Villas; one of the first properties to be built in New Filey, the Villas were subsequently enlarged on being converted to a convent school. When the school closed in 1969 it was acquired by Filey Urban District Council and eventually became the Town Hall.

37. Mr and Mrs James Robinson stand outside their Beach Cottage in September 1905.

Remarkable confidence in the rather rudimentary sea walls was exhibited by the builders of the first properties on the sea front. The building with the most unusual design is now the Ackworth Retirement Home; built as the Spa Saloon dating from the mid-19th century, it is in the Renaissance style with a mansard roof (one with parts of different pitch). Downcliffe House, a substantial stone built property, was built by John Unett, the son of John Wilkes Unett. Deepdene, close to the Coastguard Station, was at the time of its building in the early years of the century, one of Filey's largest private houses. After about half a century in private ownership it was acquired by the Council and was, for a time, a nursing home before being converted into flats. There is now a development of apartments there.

A building which made a major contribution to the life of Filey was the Grand Cinema; opened on 15th February 1911, it originally had facilities which included a café below the main entrance and a lecture room above; in addition to the screening of literally thousands of full-length films, it has been the venue for many productions of local operatic and dramatic societies, and also that of West End touring companies.

A substantial building which had a chequered career was the Royal Hotel; built about 1850, it stood in Belle Vue Street to the south of the Three Tuns. Its time as an hotel was but a few years, after which it had a variety of domestic and commercial uses before being demolished in about 1936.

Old and New Filey were, in a sense, drawn together by the building of properties on Union Street in the middle years of the 19th century. Perhaps the Street was so named because of this function. More building then soon took place in West Parade (West Road), Somerville Road (Station Road) and West Street (West Avenue); also in Chapel Street and Alma Terrace (the west and east sections of Mitford Street). What is now known as Chapel Street was then Chapel Road.

The Coastguard Station was originally situated at the sea-ward end of Queen Street (number 97) and was transferred to its present site on the Foreshore Road at the turn of the century. The houses adjacent to the present Station were for the coastguard officers.

At Enclosure in 1791, the then main street of Filey was known as Town Street; it subsequently became King Street, then Queen Street for the section east of Skelton's Lane (Reynold's Street) and finally the whole street was named Queen Street.

In the early 20th century, building took place adjacent to Station Avenue and Station Road, and along Muston Road, and Scarborough Road. In the early 1920s Filey Urban District Council began house-building with The Gardens group of houses on Scarborough Road. In the decade before World War II and in the late 1940s, more local authority housing was built in the estates then known as Newlands and Newthorpe, but now known as Grove Road, Ash Road, Ash Grove and Scarborough Road, West Road, Rowan Avenue and Hazel Road.

The building in Mitford Street which is now the Fire Station, was built and opened in 1935 as a furniture shop by Walter Wright and son-in-law Jack Fearon; before moving across the road the partners had business premises in part of the Albert Hall.

A new concept in holiday accommodation for Filey was developed shortly before World War II; this was represented by the group of bungalows built in West Vale, specifically for furnished letting in the season. They were, however, soon to be used to accommodate families evacuated from Hull and Hartlepool; they are now privately owned.

About the same time, the Brig Cinema opened and soon became an important place of entertainment for residents and members of the forces stationed in and around Filey.

During the war years almost no building for civilian purposes took place, but in the years following, land to the south-east of Muston Road was developed, both for private and local authority housing. The name given to Grange Avenue is no doubt a link either with Muston Grange Farm to the south of Filey, or with Grange Farm in Muston Road, whose buildings stood close to where is now number 2, Wharfedale. Other roads on the estate were named after people who had a connection with Filey; those commemorated were Canon Cooper, Vicar from 1880 to 1935; Ben Hindle and Welford Gofton, who were both Clerks to Filey Urban District Council, (the original name suggested for Welford Road was Prince of Wales Avenue); George Doran and Leonard Hallam were both members of the Council. Clarence Drive has a nominal link with Clarence House and the name Padbury recalls the owner of a brickworks situated nearby in the early years of the century.

A major building programme of detached and semi-detached bungalows was embarked upon in 1963 on the north-west side of Muston Road by Northern Ideal Homesteads Ltd. of Barnsley. These proved to be popular as retirement homes for new Filey residents and the infusion of energetic, newly-retired members into existing Filey societies and organisations was welcomed.

Similar developments were soon under way north of Scarborough Road and although the original plan to build almost to the cliff top was not pursued, a mixed development of bungalows and houses provided for a further significant increase in Filey's population.

A change in Filey's housing pattern was signalled in April 1961 when Bay Court Development (Filey) Limited, announced for sale, or for letting on lease, the flats and maisonettes at Royal Crescent Court, previously the Royal Crescent Hotel. The nomenclature proved acceptable and was to be used in future conversions and new buildings as in Ebor Court and Victoria Court on the Crescent, Ganton Court (Brooklands), Melville Court (South Crescent Road), St. Oswald's Court (Queen Street), Sledmere Court (Union Street) and Chapel Court (Station Avenue).

One of Filey's largest detached buildings is Clarence House (West Avenue); built as a girls' boarding school in mid-Victorian times, it was, in the 1930s, an hotel 'standing in its own grounds of approximately two and a half acres'. During World War II an Officer Cadet Training Unit was based there, and in April 1947 it was opened by the Earl of Feversham as a Y.H.A. hostel; some years later it also was converted to flats.

Another large building which no longer fulfils its original function is the one on Laundry Road where the Filey Laundry was situated. It was at one time the biggest single employer of labour in the area with about one hundred employees in the Season, when hotels and boarding houses in neighbouring towns were amongst its customers. Some temporary employees were girls on holiday from school who would be ushered out of the back door as the factory inspector entered by the front!

The power for the laundry was provided by a steam-engine at the Scarborough Road end of the building and its brightly polished brass and steelwork together with the fascination of its intricate movement delayed many children returning to school across the road.

One of Filey's most impressive buildings, whose architecture and instruction in stone are of the highest order, is Northcliffe. The house, and the stable and coach-house block to the north of Mitford Street, occupy one of the finest East Coast settings and were joined by a tunnel under 'Miss Clarke's Steps' adjacent to 'Clarke Asphalt', the area set aside for fishermen to dry their nets by Miss Elinor Clarke described in her obituary in 1905 as 'Filey's wealthiest resident'. The property was completed in 1892 to the design of W.H. Brierley, the noted York architect. Adjacent to the Coach-House Block is the building known as the Conference Hall which has been used by many organisations over the years. Its probable origin was as a gift from Miss Clarke to the local Volunteers as a Drill Hall. It is now a centre for scout groups.

The 6" Ordnance Survey Map of 1854 marks a windmill close to where is now the Junior School in West Road; it was there no longer on the map of 1894. Perhaps surprisingly, Seadale Terrace, off West Avenue, was in the parish of Muston until its transfer in 1935.

Filey is fortunate to have several groups of buildings which, though they may not be of architectural or historical significance, are well worth caring for because of the high standards employed in their construction and embellishment. Amongst such groups are the terraces of houses on West Avenue between Rutland Street and Brooklands, and, overlooking the hard tennis courts and bowling green, the terrace on Southdene; the one on the south side of Belle Vue Street, the terraces in Rutland Street, Brooklands, Station Avenue and Station Road. There are many more groups of houses, and individual ones also, which have features of stone, brick and wood which are a tribute to their architects and builders; firms responsible for many of these buildings were those of Brooks, Fells and Sawdon Brothers.

Few communities remain unchanged for long in their physical characteristics, and to this Filey is no exception. Determined efforts have rightly been made over the years to retain and enhance the architecturally good and to resist the inappropriate and unsuitable. Although mistakes have been made on both counts, many feel that Filey has still a uniqueness in its corporate whole that should be cared for and even cherished.

Listed Buildings

The following buildings have been listed by the Department of the Environment as being of special architectural or historic interest.

>Northcliffe House, Cottage, Lodge and Coachhouse.
>Church Cliff Farm; House, Buildings and Dovecote.
>St. Oswald's Church.
>Church Street; Numbers 13, 35, 41, 43 - 45.
>Queen Street; Numbers 8 - 10 (Museum), Foord's Hotel.
>The Crescent; Numbers 1 - 7, 8 - 14, 15 - 21, Royal Crescent Court, 23-28, 44.
>Rutland Street; Numbers 24 - 38.
>West Avenue; Numbers 27 - 41.
>Railway Station.

All are classified Grade II with the exception of St. Oswald's Church which is Grade I.

Old Filey

The development of New Filey, which began slowly in the 1820s and increased in pace in the 1840s and 1850s, had less effect on life in Old Filey than might have been expected. Only a few hundred yards separated the two communities and yet for many a journey from one to the other would be a rare event. Perhaps almost the only group of people which would regularly cross Murray Street would be that consisting of girls and women who lived in and around Queen Street and worked in the boarding or private houses and hotels on or near the Crescent.

There was, of course, a very real sense of a long established community in Old Filey which was not present in the new town where, in the mid-19th century the majority of residents were born outside the town. This sense of community resulted from family relationships, the physical closeness in which the members lived and the necessary dependence they had upon each other. Many men and women and young people were also united in common endeavours relating to their working and religious life and these factors served to bind them more closely together.

The building plan was also a major factor in encouraging a feeling of 'togetherness'. Queen Street was the main thoroughfare and contained a wide variety of shops supplying almost all the basic requirements of the inhabitants who lived in the street or in the many groups of dwellings, often called 'yards', which led off from the street. Census surveys give the names of these yards; the exact situation of many is however not known. These are some:

    Suggit's Yard
    Mallory Yard
    Mosey Yard
    Crawford Yard
    Richardson Yard
    Jones Yard
    Bulmer Yard
    Clifford Yard
    Dunn's Yard
    Bird's Yard
    Cammish Yard
    Lorriman's Yard
    Roulson's Yard
    Parkinson's Yard
    Crofton's Yard
    Skelton's Yard
    Stamford Yard

In some surveys they are described as 'rents', as in Mosey's Rent and Mallory's Rent, possibly indicating the owners of the properties; in other cases the names seem to refer either to the builders or one of the residents.

There are now few places where anything remains of these groups of dwellings; almost all the houses have been demolished and the sites built over. Wenlock Place, off Church Hill, has the not untypical narrow access which led to nine dwellings (as shown on the 25" Ordnance Survey Map of 1894) and in which, according to the 1851 Census, nearly sixty people lived. Other entries can still be seen as between 61 and 63 Queen Street to White's Yard, between 75 and 77 to Richardson's Yard and 81 and 83 to Stockdale's Yard. Other places listed in the Census Returns for Old Filey in 1851 and 1861 include Victoria Passage, Stephenson Lane and Ocean Place. Eleven families were also able in 1851 to give Trafalgar Square as their address, and in 1841 five families lived in the more modern sounding Manor Court.

A glimpse into a balanced cohesive society is afforded by considering the employment of many Queen Street residents in 1851; in addition to the fishermen, fish curers, fish merchants, fish mongers and rope makers one would expect to see, there were also, Mary Jenkinson Story who made straw hats, Rachel Cammish a dairy maid, Davison Philliskirk a master saddler and Robert Pinder who was a watchmaker. Other jobs listed include joiner, cordwainer (shoemaker), ostler, farmer, baker, plasterer, brick-maker, washerwoman and confectioner. In this year Queen Street had 96 houses of which 89 were occupied.

An inconsequential detail concerning Queen Street revealed by the 1851 Census, is the popularity of Elizabeth as a Christian name. Of the first 52 entries of individual dwellings, just half listed at least one resident of that name, giving a total of 30 girls or women who answered to Elizabeth or one of the many diminutives. Most of the surnames were ones still thought of as 'old' Filey names. An analysis of the 1841 Census suggests that the most frequently occurring surnames were: Cammish, for which there were 17 families; Jenkinson 13; Simpson, 9; Robinson, Richardson and Cowling, 7; Willis and Crawford 6; Cappleman, Scales and Skelton with 5 family entries. By 1871 a change of order had taken place with 21 family entries under Jenkinson, 13 for Cammish, 8 for Cappleman and Haxby, 6 for Cowling, 5 for Pashby and 4 for Scales and Ross.

A job analysis of the 1841 records for the whole of Filey indicates that there were about 130 fishermen, 57 agricultural labourers, 61 female servants, 13 sailors, 8 bricklayers and 7 brickmakers, 2 ship owners and representatives of about 45 other occupations. In 1881, the pattern of employment was very similar to 1841; however, there were now several categories associated with the railway which arrived in 1846; 4 clerks, 4 porters, 1 gateman, 1 platelayer, 1 signalman and 1 inspector. Other occupiers of more unusual employment included a goldminer, a tea-planter, a basket maker and a bathing maid who was 64 years old!

The cohesive strength of a community can be gauged by assessing the way in which it faces adversity and because it has had for centuries a very close link with one of the recognisably most dangerous professions, Filey has many times found itself in just such a situation The loss through storm of nets, sails and boats was an economic blow to fishermen and boat owners and recovery would take months and even years. Of more tragic consequence were the gales which resulted in loss of life. In days long before health insurance and social security it was necessary for a community to care for its own and those who lived here then did so with compassion. The widows were supported and the newly-orphaned would perhaps be brought up by branches of the extended family so that the mother could go out to work. The opening of funds to enable fishermen to replace lost fishing gear, or to provide a small pension for widows was a not infrequent occurrence. One such occasion was the storm of October 1869 during which all the 31 yawls associated with Filey lost nets. Following the exceptional gale of October 1880, an appeal was made by the newly arrived Vicar, the Rev. A.N. Cooper, to which by February 1881 the impressive sum of

£1090 had been donated. £700 of this was set aside to provide allowances of four to eight shillings per week to each of those who had been widowed, and the remainder was used for special cases of need and for the replacement of nets.

Winters could be long and hard when catches were poor and charity soup kitchens were an important facility for hungry school-children. The provision merchant who supplied groceries to customers over many weeks on deferred payment was a god-send to families whose weekly income might have fallen to nothing. The 3-acre lake at Primrose Valley was constructed in just such a winter in 1910 by unemployed yawl fishermen for local landowner, Cllr. R. Smith, who wished to help the community by providing much needed employment.

Institutions associated with Old Filey in mid-Victorian times of course included Parish Church and Methodist Chapel; also available were several inns, some of which still remain. Those which are no longer to be seen in Queen Street include the Ship Inn (number 78); the Pack Horse, which was thatched and eventually replaced by the Crown Hotel; the Britannia, which stood on the site between where are now numbers 65 and 71. The Hope and Anchor was situated in Church Street facing down Queen Street; it was demolished in 1891. Another important institution in the community was the Post Office which through the 1840s and 1850s was situated at number 79 Queen Street. It was later to be found for a few years at the corner of Queen Street and Reynold's Street (then King Street and Skelton's Lane). Occasions on which the Post Office was particularly important included those following severe storms when intense anxiety was experienced for the safety of those caught at sea. One such gale occurred in 1867 after which seven yawls were missing. Families gathered at the telegraph office to wait for news and after several anxious hours news was received that six yawls were safe in the Humber; three further hours later the telegraph clerk received the welcome message that the seventh had also reached a safe haven.

It is a tribute to the underlying strength of the Old Filey community that a tangible sense of unity has survived so many years during which physical closeness has been steadily diminished as families moved from old properties to new estates; also many of its members have moved from the town to be replaced by others entering and becoming part of its continuing life. The many shops in Queen Street on which the community depended have long since closed, the Yards and Rents are all demolished and many have been replaced by new houses and flats; the old, low stone fishermen's cottages which formed often a subject for artists have gone, to be replaced by bungalows. St. Oswald's Court stands now where previously was the Vicarage in its spacious grounds. However, much of the old street remains, and with it sufficient of its atmosphere to enable those who will, to recall or to imagine it as it was when it bustled with the life of a vigorous, independent community.

The Anglican Churches

By a margin of several centuries, St. Oswald's Parish Church is the oldest of Filey's buildings. One of the largest and most impressive churches in the district, it is stone built with a chancel, central tower, transepts, clerestoried nave and north and south porches. Not surprisingly, considering its age, the early history of the church is uncertain. The evidence of the building itself suggests that its construction took place over a period of about 50 years commencing in the late 12th century. Many churches of this period leave unanswered questions and Filey is no exception. Why, and at which point in its construction was the plan for a west tower changed to one which included a tower over the crossing? The evidence for this change is in the very substantial piers and responds at the west end which were clearly intended to support a tower. Perhaps the alteration in plan was because of the failure of the pier close to the font; this pier leans perceptibly. Unusually, the chancel floor is two steps lower than the remainder of the church. There are clear indications on all four faces of the tower that an earlier roof was more steeply pitched, perhaps because it was thatched. It is believed the roof was lowered towards the end of the 14th century.

A small stone figure is built into the wall of the south aisle; local tradition suggests it is of a boy bishop although an alternative explanation is that it represents a canon of Bridlington Priory.

An Early English Sedilia seat and a piscina (used for cleaning the vessels after Holy Communion) in the south transept suggest that perhaps the monks of Bridlington Priory, being Augustinian and therefore expected to celebrate mass separately from the people, did so in this transept. The transepts were, until the mid-19th century, separated from the body of the church by walls and were known as St. Mary's and St. Oswald's Chapels.

Other work believed to have been carried out in the 14th century, included raising the walls of the nave aisles and erecting the parapets. The five bay arcades have pointed arches and the columns are alternately octagonal and round.

The South Door is an excellent example of late Norman work with a semi-circular arch of four orders and the mouldings and arch of the Priest's Door on the south side of the chancel indicate that it is Early English work of about 1230. Close to the Priest's Door on the wall near the sundial is a Mass Clock marked for the times for Mass in pre-Reformation times. The oak doors in the south porch are a memorial to the Rev Percy Vernon Corner who was Vicar from 1937 to 1967.

The stone altar in the sanctuary was recovered this century from the chancel floor where presumably it had been placed at the Reformation in the 16th century. This would have been done deliberately to take away its significance in worship. Until the Reformation it would presumably be close to the place to

38. The Priest's door at St Oswald's Church.

which it has now been returned. Its age is uncertain and may indeed be from the church which preceded St. Oswald's.

In 1839 the screen across the chancel was removed and the walls whitewashed. According to Canon Cooper the small figure on the south wall was only saved with seconds to spare as a workman was about to demolish it with a pick-axe.

In 1883 fund raising began for a comprehensive scheme of renovations and work began in 1885. Considerable work was done on the north aisle wall, the transepts, the nave roof and the floor. The old beams in the roof were found to be in a particularly poor state and there were revealed signs that there once had been a door in the south transept. The total cost of these improvements was £4400 for the building and £370 for new furniture and fittings.

Surprisingly for a church of the size and apparent importance of Filey, only relatively recently has it had its own vicarage. In the early 12th century the Church which preceded St. Oswald's was part of Walter de Gant's foundation endowment of Bridlington Priory and priests from there served the church in succeeding centuries. After the Dissolution of the Monasteries in the 1530s, the living became a perpetual curacy. In 1743 the curacy was supplied by the Vicar of Folkton and some years later it was the Vicar of Hunmanby who provided the curate for St. Oswald's.

The administration of the Parish Church in Filey had some unusual features. In the appointment of churchwardens usually one was chosen by the incumbent and one by the parishioners; however, in Filey, both were chosen by the people. This arrangement was challenged by the Rev. Evan Williams in 1820 and the law suit which followed found in favour of established tradition; it did however, cost the people £90. The better relations which existed between the people and the Rev. A.N. Cooper were indicated by the fact that when in 1881 he was offered the opportunity to nominate he declined. The procedure so jealously guarded by Filey parishioners is now the established way of appointing churchwardens.

In the early days of the 19th century music was provided by two violinists and a cellist. A very serious fire occurred in 1908 which resulted in considerable damage including the destruction of the organ which was situated at the west end of the Church. The new organ, built by Binns of Leeds was installed in November 1908 at a cost of £900. A major programme of repairs, renovations and improvements began in the late 1970s and still continues.

Sadly little is known today of those who ministered at the Church's services from its foundation until the early 19th century. However, we do know a little about the Rev. Evan Williams who was Perpetual Curate from 1809 to 1833. By any standards an eccentric man, it is recorded that he would buy on the coble landing a shilling's worth of fish and when that was finished return for more; his milk was delivered to him in a pitcher which he let down from a

39. The nave of St Oswald's Church.

bedroom window at the end of a rope. The Church House at this time was at 33, Church Street. He would not allow a woman into the house and for some reason preferred to enter and leave through a window rather than the door. On occasion, soon after commencing a service, he would announce that there would be no sermon, and then depart rapidly, locking the door behind him. No wonder relations between himself and his parishioners were a little strained.

Mr. Williams was followed by the Rev. Thomas Norfolk Jackson who ministered acceptedly for forty years and who died on the same day as the Rev. A.N. Cooper was married; the church bells rang out in commemoration and celebration at an interval of only a few hours.

In June 1873, Mr. Jackson's successor, the Rev. Basil R. Wood, 'read himself in' at St. Oswald's; this consisted of reading before the congregation the 39 Articles of the Anglican Church. In the evening he preached in the newly completed St. John's Church to his parishioners who listened 'with deep interest and breathless attention' to his address which 'was full of the kindliest feeling towards all classes'; an auspicious start indeed. His incumbency however, was to last only seven years.

Mr. Wood's successor in 1880 was the remarkable Arthur Neville Cooper who was Vicar of Filey for 55 years. Born in 1850 he began his working life as a clerk at Somerset House and developed his love of walking as he made his way to work each day through several central London parks. He came to Filey following a curacy in Chester-le-Street and his obituary reported that almost his first task was to raise funds on behalf of the families of many local fishermen lost by storm at sea. He proved himself on this and subsequent occasions an able worker for charity. A liked and respected incumbent he became more widely known as a result of his long walks and the books he wrote about them. His first stroll was to London, which, after leaving Filey following Sunday evening service, he reached by Saturday lunch time averaging about 35 miles each day, in time to return home by train to take morning service the following day. On Easter Monday 1887, he set off on foot for Hull, going on from there to Rotterdam. On disembarking, and travelling in as straight a line as possible, he averaged about 30 miles per day to reach Rome in one month. He enjoyed walking on the Continent and during a walking career of about 30 years he reached on foot, Budapest, Monte Carlo, Barcelona, Copenhagen, Stockholm, Lourdes and Vienna.

The books about his travels were written in a light, humorous, easily readable style. He carried little in his knapsack beside a change of underwear and in one book about his walk to Rome, he recounts how he arrived in Hamelyn having been drenched in a storm; his evening was consequently spent wearing a skirt and petticoat borrowed from the manageress of the hotel in which he was staying. Fortunately, he was the only guest. Another small problem he encountered nearer home was reported in the local press in September 1884. During the course of a wedding ceremony at St. Oswald's, the best man held the bride's hand so intently that Mr. Cooper assumed he was the bridegroom until a guest pointed out his error. Canon Cooper has a road on the Grange Avenue estate named after him.

Canon Cooper's long incumbency was followed by the very short tenure of the Rev. R.S. Dawson whose stay in Filey was to last only 18 months.

Generations of Filey churchgoers must have wondered, especially on stormy winter nights, why the Parish Church was built on the north side of the Church Ravine when the people lived on the south side. There is no certain answer to this question but one suggestion is that church founders sometimes thought it advisable that a contemplative walk precede church attendance.

As Filey expanded towards the south the need for a second Anglican church became apparent for two reasons. The increased population, especially in the summer, placed a strain on the seating capacity of St. Oswald's and many now lived or stayed a considerable distance from the church.

For residents of, and visitors to, New Filey, the Iron Church was erected in 1857 on the east side of West Avenue midway between Brooklands and Southdene. Built without endowment it could accommodate about 350 worshippers. In 1860 the incumbent was the Rev. G.W. Longstaff.

Opened in 1871 as a chapel-of-ease to replace the Iron Church, the Church of St. John the Evangelist was built in stone in 13th century style with nave, chancel and transepts. The cost of the chancel and its furnishings was met by 'the Ladies of Filey' who raised funds by sales of work; visitors also made considerable contributions.

In late Victorian times all four main Filey churches would be comfortably filled on Sundays during the Season. However, by the middle years of the 20th century St. John's was little used for worship. It was later to enjoy a new lease of life when in the 1970s an ambitious programme of alterations and refurbishment saw the building converted to a smaller but well used church and a much needed church hall.

Methodism

Methodism came relatively late to Filey; perhaps that is one of the reasons why when it did, its impact and its lasting effect were considerable. John and Charles Wesley were the remarkable sons of the Rev. Samuel Wesley, the Rector of Epworth in Lincolnshire. John was born there in 1703 and Charles in 1707; there were 17 other children of whom 8 survived to reach adult life. Both John and Charles graduated from Oxford University where they, together with others, were so methodical in their devotions and charitable endeavours that they acquired the nick-name 'Methodists'. Soon after returning from church work in the American Colonies, John found himself deeply moved at a church service in London in 1738 and embarked upon a lifetime of forthright evangelism which was to have a major effect on the religious and social fabric of the British Isles.

Charles also was much affected on the same occasion and made an incalculable contribution through the hymns he composed, many of which are still sung Sunday by Sunday throughout the world.

John's life was long and full of dramatic incident as he travelled, usually by horse, in all weathers and on roads good and bad, covering between 4,000 and 5,000 miles each year Often preaching several times in a day, he spoke directly to more hearers than any other English 18th century cleric. He visited Bridlington regularly about every two years between 1770 and 1790 and also preached in Scarborough at a chapel just below St. Mary's Church on at least a dozen occasions. Though coming close to Filey, he records in his diary of having passed through Hunmanby in June 1774, there is no indication that John Wesley visited Filey.

Though few details are available regarding early Methodism in Filey, it is probable that the first work and witness took place about 1806. A small Society belonging to the Wesleyan branch of the Methodist Church was formed in 1810 with the first Chapel being opened in 1811. This was in what is now Mitford Street but was then known as Back Lane before its name was changed to Chapel Street. The site was where now stands the Elderly Persons' Club and the building was used until the 1940s as a corn shop.

The very early years of Methodism in Filey were difficult ones with little success and much opposition. A significant aspect of early Methodist tradition was that of preaching in the streets, but this proved unwelcome to some of the residents who made their feelings known by pelting the preachers sufficiently vigorously with dried fish to cause blood to flow. When the few adherents met in a shed with the intention of holding a service, their devotions were, on at least one occasion, disrupted by pigs being driven in amongst them. By 1823 there were just 15 members in the Wesleyan Society.

In March 1823, however, there began in Filey what has been described as 'The Great Change'. This was very largely occasioned by the arrival in the town of John Oxtoby. Born near Pocklington in 1762, he joined the Wesleyan Methodists in 1799 and later became associated with the Primitive Methodist cause in Bridlington. Early in 1823 at a meeting there, the members who for some time had been trying to establish a Primitive Methodist Society in Filey, were on the point of taking a decision to give up because it was felt that Filey was a hopeless cause. But John Oxtoby declared that there was a great work to do there and asked for one more chance. This was agreed and soon he was on the road to Filey. A passer-by reported seeing him deep in prayer on Mill Hill before entering the town. His prayers were answered and soon people listened and responded to his call. The effect on Filey was remarkable and the character of the town changed. Whereas once it was described as a fishing place of great notoriety, it became known for the uprightness of its inhabitants. Canon Cooper wrote of the town being 'turned upside down'.

The Primitive Methodist cause was soon strong enough to require premises and the Bethesda Chapel was built in 1823 and registered in the following year. It stood where is now the Salvation Army Hall.

The steady increase in the numbers of Primitive Methodists is indicated by the building of extensions to the Chapel in 1843 and 1859. In his short history of the Primitive Methodist movement in Filey, Frank Hanson records that financial assistance for the later extension was given by John Crossley, the Halifax carpet manufacturer; this suggests that some visitors were becoming part of the fabric of life in Old Filey as well as in the New.

However, by 1865 the need for a completely new building was becoming apparent, and at a meeting on 20th November the decision was taken to begin fund raising with a Halibut Supper at the close of the following spring fishing. In September 1867, negotiations were begun in order to acquire a site in Union Street, and arrangements were made for 200,000 bricks to be supplied. A considerable sum of money was needed, most of which would come from the fishing community which was to suffer much material loss at sea as a result of the October 1869 gale — so severe was the storm that it was regarded as a miracle that not one fisherman was lost.

Many difficulties had been overcome when the foundation stone for a new Chapel to seat 900 people was laid on 5th July 1870 by Mrs. Ellis of Grimsby who donated the pitch pine for the new building. The opening ceremony on 18th June 1871 was the first of many great occasions that were to take place there over the next one hundred and more years.

The annual Good Friday fish suppers were memorable events; in April 1881, 360 sat down together, and the account in the Filey Post of the fish feast of April 1906 is so vividly recorded that it deserves repeating.

> "...When all is done, the dishes are taken to the Primitive Methodist Chapel, the largest building in the town, and there set out in a display of bewildering diversity. Huge cods, cooked whole, and stuffed; steaks crumbed; fish inside fish to mingle flavours, like the ortolans of the Regent Phillip; fish fritters, fish swimming in sauces, stranded in batter, caught fast in crust; buttered, lemoned, flavoured with ham — how shall the tale be told? Great pies challenge small pies, whilst crabs and lobsters cheerfully rubicund, hold out their pincer claws, in amity, as though inviting the honour of being tasted. These crabs and lobsters give no trouble to the eater — every part has been skilfully laid open for picking, and even the dyspeptic finds it hard to resist their charms. But the king among them all is the Seven-Decker. A great erection of piecrust, enclosing alternate layers of varied fish and bacon. There is nothing to beat fish cooked in this way, and had the secret been out in the time of Queen Elizabeth, Her Puissant Majesty would never have had to issue her edict for compulsory fish-eating days."

Another great day must have been the one in June 1891 when 1000 people came from Hull in two special trains to share in a service at Ebenezer as a gesture of appreciation for the work and witness in Hull of bands of Filey fishermen.

The stamina of Victorian Methodists was impressive as indicated by the programme for the Railway Servants Camp Meeting at Filey on Sunday, July 11th 1880. The adherents began with prayer at 7.00 a.m. at Ebenezer followed by addresses there at 9.00 a.m. The remainder of the morning was occupied with addresses at the Cliff Top and other parts of the town. After refreshments, the supporters processed to New Filey where they listened to more addresses. The procession then made its way to the Camp Ground where six more addresses were delivered. Avid, apparently, for yet more of the spoken word, at 5.00 p.m. they made their way to King Street in the Old Town. To round off the day the stalwarts were at last able to sit down for the religious experience meeting which began at 6.00 p.m. at Ebenezer. The singing, an integral part of this somewhat strenuous day, was conducted by Messrs. J. & M. Haxby.

In 1901 a disastrous fire destroyed the organ and caused considerable damage to the fabric of the building. The new instrument subsequently installed was recognised as one of the finest church organs in the district.

Ebenezer was a centre of activity through the week and its influence permeated much of life in Filey, particularly in the older part of the town. It was said of William Jenkinson, a devoted servant of the Chapel, that he could see a hundred of his relatives in chapel on Sunday. Another much respected fisherman member was Jenkinson Haxby who gave '60 years active Christian service'.

In the early 1970s it was becoming apparent that there was much to recommend the uniting of the two Methodist congregations, and in 1975 Ebenezer closed after 104 years of witness. The final Sunday Services were on 4th May when the President of the Methodist Conference, Rev. J. Russell Pope, conducted the Morning Service.

The Filey Fishermen's Choir, for long very closely associated with Ebenezer Chapel, enjoys still a high reputation for its singing mainly gospel songs. Always warmly welcomed on its frequent engagements throughout Yorkshire, it continues a tradition begun over a century ago.

In the late 1830s the Wesleyans, having found their premises inadequate, built a new chapel in Murray Street in 1839, on a site opposite to where is now Mills supermarket. This served the Wesleyans well, but an increasing chapel congregation encouraged members to build new premises with a spire rising to 90 feet at the junction of Union Street and Station Avenue. On completion, the congregation moved and the Murray Street building became the Victoria Rooms. Opened in 1876, Trinity was another great Methodist centre of work and witness until January 1918 when a disastrous fire, whose cause was never established, destroyed most of the building. A vigorous rebuilding campaign soon began and on March 7th 1923 the new chapel was re-opened.

40. Harvest Festival at the Ebenezer Chapel about 1920.

The ceremonies included the opening at 2.30 p.m. of the Schoolroom door and the Chapel door by Cllr William Gofton and Mrs James Ellis respectively, a service at 3 00 p m conducted by the Rev Dr J T Wardle Stafford, was followed by tea at 4.30 p.m. and a 'Great Public Meeting' chaired by the Rt Hon T R Ferens of Hull.

Strangely, about the same time as the fire at Trinity, the Victoria Hall was similarly destroyed; the cause of this fire too, was never ascertained.

When the two congregations united, the use of the name Trinity was discontinued and the building became known as the Filey Methodist Church, where the work begun nearly two hundred years ago still continues.

St Mary's

One of the most attractive and satisfying buildings in Filey is St Mary's Catholic Church in Brooklands. Built by Sawdon Brothers to the design of Father E. Roulin, it was opened on 10th May 1906, just eight months and one day after the laying of the foundation stone. Father Eugene Roulin, a French Benedictine monk, was the first resident Roman Catholic priest in Filey having been sent here from Ampleforth Abbey as a chaplain to the Sisters of Charity. The Sisters were nuns who in 1904 established the Convent of the Sacred Heart in John Street. Both inside and out, the church amply repays closer examination; the monograms on the turret are splendidly fashioned and inside there is a wealth of detailed work, much of it, like the church itself, to the design of Father Roulin.

An unusual ceremony took place in September 1908 when on the occasion of the Eucharistic Congress in London, under a canopy supported by four men, the Blessed Sacrament was carried in procession around the church led by nuns singing the *Pange Lingua*. A less solemn event held the previous month in the Victoria Hall, was a Spanish Festivity; opened by the Duchess of Norfolk, its purpose was to raise funds to pay off the £500 debt still remaining on the church. The Festivity President was Mark Sykes of Sledmere Hall who, in his address, attributed Britain's greatness to the challenge presented to it by the Spanish Armada. Two, no doubt well patronised, fund-raisers were the Laughing Curiosity Room looked after by Miss M. Watkins and the Character Readings of Professor Khan Tellum.

The absence in Filey of a Roman Catholic church had long been felt by both residents and visitors, and St. Mary's was warmly welcomed into Filey's religious life. Congregational needs in post-war summer seasons resulted in the opening in 1961 of a well-designed and integrated church extension.

Salvation Army

The Filey Corps of the Salvation Army continues to play an important part in the religious and social life of Filey. For over fifty years it has served the needs of the people from its present Hall and from the Albert Hall which stood on the same site until 1974 when it was replaced by the new building; before moving to Mitford Street the Corps was based in the old Methodist Day School building (now Dixon T.V.). The open air meetings of witness led by the Corps with musical accompaniment were a familiar feature of Filey's everyday life for many years.

Other Religious Groups

The Christian Science Society for many years maintained premises in Rutland Street where it held services and provided facilities for passers-by to read scriptural passages.

Groups which have ceased to meet in Filey include the Plymouth Brethren who used the Albert Hall from late Victorian times until the 1930s and in later years premises in Belle Vue Street; the Christian Army also met in the Albert Hall for a time.

The Society of Friends, Quakers, maintained a presence in Filey from mid-Victorian days through to the 1920s using premises in West Avenue and Rutland Street. They were not the first in Filey of this persuasion as in Archbishop Herring's Visitation Returns of 1743 it was reported that the only dissenters here were the members of a family of Quakers. Friends now living in Filey worship at Beverley Meeting House.

The Railway

The development of railway systems was one of the great transforming influences throughout the world on life in the 19th century. Much of the inventive genius required for its development was provided by British engineers and in Great Britain the rapidity with which the system spread across the land is a measure of the energy and financial resources of the early Victorians.

In Yorkshire, Leeds and Hull had been linked by rail in 1840. Surprisingly, a line between Whitby and Pickering had been built four years earlier than this, though horses provided the motive power until locomotives were introduced in 1847.

In Filey the arrival of the railway was awaited with considerable interest and enthusiasm, particularly amongst those who were concerned either with the very old business of fishing, or the new one of catering for visitors. The railway was to prove of vital importance in transporting fish to all parts of the U.K., and in bringing increasing numbers of people to Filey for holidays by the

41. A late Victorian view of the Railway Station.

sea. There is nothing to suggest that anyone in Filey was quite as cynical as the resident of a nearby resort who published a pamphlet which included the opinion that 'Scarborough has no wish for a greater influx of vagrants and those who have no money to spend'. In spite of such sentiments the line from York to Scarborough opened on 7th July 1845.

George Hudson obtained an Act of Parliament in the same year to join Seamer, Filey and Bridlington by rail, and the section from Seamer to Filey opened for traffic on 5th October 1846.

In the southern part of the East Riding there had also been rapid developments. A line had been built to link Selby and Hull in 1840 and the operating company soon began to plan a line from Hull to Bridlington. These proposals came to fruition just one day after the opening of the line from Seamer to Filey.

The section from Bridlington to Filey through the Wolds presented the engineers with considerable challenges. A long embankment of gradually increasing height begins soon after leaving Bridlington Station, which, near Sewerby, is followed by two deep cuttings before Bempton is reached. The line continues to rise to its highest point of just over 100m and then has a long downhill run which incorporates more embankments and cuttings before Hunmanby is reached. Not surprisingly, these engineering works required considerable time to complete and the section between Bridlington and Filey was not publicly opened until 20th October 1847.

Filey could now be reached in a day from almost all parts of the country and it became an increasingly popular seaside resort.

The railway continued to play an essential part in the life of the community in a wide variety of ways. Until road haulage replaced much of the rail freight traffic, a large goods shed stood where now is Silver Birches. A long wagon siding extended from the up line almost as far as the main road along what is now the boundary between Silver Birches and Station Garage. A coal siding was built between the line and the Gas Works and was much used in supplying coal for domestic consumption and gas manufacture. Goods traffic to and through Filey finally ceased in the mid-1960s.

The line through Filey had for long the distinction of being one of the longest sections without a junction anywhere on the whole English rail network. This section was from Seamer to Driffield. However, this ceased to be when the triangular section to Butlin's Camp opened on 10th May 1947. Here, the new station had four 900 foot long platforms and saw arrivals from, and departures to, many of the main centres of population including London, Manchester and Edinburgh. After the turntable at Scarborough was removed the triangle was used for several years to turn around occasional steam locomotive visitors to Scarborough.

In April 1968 a closure notice for the Hull to Seamer line was issued and a strong and effective campaign was mounted to prevent closure taking place.

Following a public enquiry in Bridlington on 21st November 1968, the notice was withdrawn to the relief of many occasional and regular users of the line.

In the late 1950s diesel multiple units (d.m.u.s.) began to replace steam locomotive-hauled trains between Hull and Scarborough, although for several years more summer Saturday excursion trains to Newcastle, Leeds Leicester, Manchester and other large towns continued to be steam-hauled.

In order to save maintenance costs the section between Hunmanby and Bridlington was changed to single track working in the late 1970s. Several years later the section between Filey and Seamer was similarly changed. It now became necessary for the approximately ten trains per day in each direction to be carefully timed to pass between Filey and Hunmanby.

Gradual replacement of the long serving d.m.u.s. by Sprinter and Pacer units began in 1987 and by 1988 Filey had the quickest and most frequent services between Hull and Scarborough in its 140 year railway history.

In 1988 the station staff was reduced to one man whose shift ended in mid-afternoon, after which the station was unmanned. This situation may be compared with that at the turn of the century when, in addition to the Station Master, there were several clerks and porters as well as staff for a refreshment room and a branch of W. H. Smith and Sons.

Education

The availability of elementary education in a village prior to the 19th century was frequently a matter of chance and often simply dependent upon there being someone who might feel able to instruct a few pupils for a very small charge.

In Filey in 1595, the curate was reported to be teaching without a licence. Most probably his class would be held in St. Oswald's Church. In Hunmanby, in 1636, a few pupils were taught by the parish clerk whose classroom was the parish church. In 1743, of 168 East Riding parishes making Visitation Returns to Archbishop Herring, 101 had no school. The Returns on Education of The Poor indicate for Filey a school attendance of between 40 and 50 in 1819, and in 1831 a Church of England National School was first held 'inconveniently' in a Methodist Chapel.

W.S. Cortis (1860) refers to the Church School as being built in 1839 and enlarged in 1846 with a mixed schoolroom on the ground floor and an infants' room above. This building apparently was in Scarborough Road and was replaced in 1874 by a new National School on the same site.

Filey's rapidly growing population continued to place increasing pressure on the school and it was enlarged in 1892. However, the accommodation soon again proved insufficient and the Vicar, Canon Cooper, initiated fund-raising schemes which in a short time resulted in the opening in1900 of the Infants' School in Mitford Street (where now stands Sledmere

42. End-of-term for pupils at Mr. J. H. Daniel's private school, South Crescent. The school later transferred to Southcliffe, Primrose Valley.

Court). The design of this new building was of a large central hall with classrooms on two sides. The ceilings were remarkable for their height and the hall must have seemed cavernous to a 3-year old pupil.

The Methodists established a school in 1842 in West Avenue, close to the Wesleyan Chapel in Murray Street, and to meet the requirements of a rising population, new premises were built in 1857. These are now occupied by Dixons T.V.

In 1908, spacious premises were built in West Road and began life as the Council School. The Methodists now saw no necessity to maintain separate educational provision and closed their school. Parents could now choose between the Church of England schools in Mitford Street and Scarborough Road, and the Council School in West Road. Not surprisingly there was a degree of rivalry between pupils in the two educational avenues. School started for some as early in life as 3 years old and almost everyone went home for dinner.

A particular strain was experienced by the schools in Autumn 1939 with the arrival in Filey of several hundred evacuees. The challenge was met by half-day schooling; local children attending one week in the morning and evacuee children in the afternoon with the sessions being reversed the following week. This arrangement was not unpopular with local children. However, within a few weeks the number of evacuees had fallen to a point where full-time schooling was available for all.

1946 saw a major change in Filey's educational system. The two alternative streams were combined with infants commencing their schooldays at the school in Mitford Street, from there going on to the Junior School at the Scarborough Road premises and finally to Secondary School in West Road, or, by selection, to Bridlington. In 1961, new buildings were provided in Muston Road and these became the Secondary School. A general move then took place as the Mitford Street premises closed, the infants moved to Scarborough Road and the juniors to West Road. In January 1988, the Infants School moved to new premises in Padbury Avenue and educational provision ceased in Scarborough Road after a span of almost 150 years.

Established over the years were several small private schools and academies, usually on or close to the Crescent. Two of the earliest were, in 1854, Miss Stephens's Ladies' Academy at 6 Rutland Terrace, and Mr. Gardiner's Boarding Academy next door at No.4. In the early 1900s, Mrs. Holmes and Miss Holmes received 'a limited number of Young Ladies to Board and Educate' at Brookville, The Crescent. The largest private boys' school was Southcliffe, established in Primrose Valley in 1901 and one of the first buildings on what was known as the Long Whins Estate. It was a Preparatory School with a wide range of facilities under the headship of J.H. Daniel. The crocodile of boys proceeding along the beach for church service was a familiar pre-W.W.I sight. The building became a hotel and is now part of the Primrose Valley holiday complex.

Another large private school was that of Miss McCallum at Clarence House, West Avenue, who was assisted by 'a large and highly qualified staff including resident French and German mistresses'. A broad curriculum included modern languages, botany and wood-carving. It also subsequently became an hotel 'in its own grounds of approximately two and a half acres'. A service establishment during W.W.II, it afterwards became a Youth Hostel and is now converted into flats.

A school mainly for very young local children was Miss Horsfield's Blue Bird School at Crescent Hill House. Opened before W.W.II it was regarded with much affection by local people.

The most important private school to be opened in Filey was the Girls' school of the Convent of the Sacred Heart in John Street. The Sisters of Charity established the Convent in 1904 and the school in the following year. Two years later the houses previously known as South Cliff Villas were purchased and the school extended. In addition to day pupils from Filey and neighbouring towns and villages, the school also had many boarders and during its 64 years became a well regarded educational establishment. The nuns of the Convent became familiar and well-liked figures and the closing of the Convent and the School in 1969 caused much regret in the town. The property was purchased by Filey Urban District Council and is now known as the Evron Centre with the former gymnasium being converted to the Concert Hall.

The Press

For a small community, Filey has been well served with local newspapers over a long period. The impetus for its first paper was, not surprisingly, the increasing number of visitors who were coming to stay during the season. A major feature of resort newspapers during the latter half of the 19th century was the list of visitors. These lists were frequently very comprehensive and in Filey's case would include not only those staying on the Crescent and the Foreshore Road, but also visitors who had found accommodation in Union Street, West Parade, Station Road and other parts of the town. At the height of the season the list would fill a whole page and would require several minutes reading by anyone recently arrived on holiday who wished to know who might be encountered on a stroll through the Crescent Gardens.

The most substantial and longest established local paper was the Filey Post and Weekly List of Visitors; this was published from 1865 to 1918. Unfortunately, the amount of Filey news in it was small and during some extensive periods there would be almost no local news at all; many quite significant events that occurred in Filey were not mentioned. One reason was that for half its life it was published in Driffield and consequently contained more news pertaining to that area of the East Riding. There was also a high proportion of national and international news and the back page contained many reports of the more violent happenings in society with accidents, murders and hangings described in a wealth of detail that today would be thought excessive. It was printed on good quality paper and copies well over a century old remain in excellent condition. The advertisements, particularly in the older editions, make intriguing reading.

Another publication, the Filey Advertiser, first appeared in 1863 under the direction of A. Halliday, but apparently was printed initially for only a few years; it re-emerged on August 4th 1876 as The Advertiser and List of Visitors at Filey, printed and published by Walter Unwin at his General Steam Printing Works, Rutland Street, for a short run. The later publication contained, in addition to visitors' lists, local information, advertisements, correspondence and summaries of sermons preached the previous Sunday.

The first local newspaper was the Filey Chronicle and Weekly List of Visitors. This was first published in 1855 and had a life only of a few years.

After the Filey Post ceased publication in 1918 several years were to elapse before the town again had a local newspaper. In February 1931, Lister Reekie, who had first come to Filey as a pierrot, brought into being the Filey News. This was also published weekly and was regarded with affection and read avidly for the Editor's pithy comments on Filey, its residents and visitors.

During a period as a member of Filey Urban District Council he was always ready to continue Council debates in the columns of his paper; a classic case of (almost) always getting the last word. The Filey News was issued for 1264 editions until May 1955 when it was absorbed by the Scarborough Mercury.

After an interval of eighty years the town had once again a Filey Advertiser; this time it was a monthly paper and 70 editions were published between April 1957 and January 1963 by John Rowland Cammish, and John and Joe Winship. Another monthly paper, the Filey and District Free Press, published by Joe Winship, proudly announced on its mast-head 'This is a British Newspaper'; it was issued 143 times between February 1963 and December 1974. These monthly newspapers, though small in scale, met a real need in the town and are much missed.

Although not as specifically local in character as those mentioned, the Scarborough Evening News and Scarborough Mercury are newspapers which are valued for their high standards of printing and publishing, as well as for their wealth of local and national news; they are supplemented by one free paper, the Top Trader.

43. Gathering news from George 'Bunny' Scales, Billy Robinson and George 'Baltic' Boynton is Lister Reekie, Editor of 'The Filey News'.

Elections

By Victorian standards, contemporary elections and election meetings are almost always very quiet affairs. 19th century elections were often regarded not just as the means by which members of Parliament were elected, but also as a welcome form of entertainment as well as, for some, an appreciated occasional addition to their incomes.

One hundred and seventy years ago the proportion of adults eligible to vote was very small. Even after the Reform Act of 1832 only about 1 in 20 of the adult population had that right. However, a much higher proportion would take the opportunity to share in the excitement which would often be generated at elections, the candidates at which were almost always either Whig (Liberal) or Tory (Conservative).

Filey had its share of lively meetings during elections in the Buckrose constituency and one of the most memorable must surely have been the one that took place at the Victoria Hall in July 1892. The Tory candidate was Mr. Clarence Goff and the Chairman was a local man, Mr. C.G. Wheelhouse. They were well supported by a 48-strong platform party but were clearly opposed by a much larger group. The hall was packed to the doors and the whistling, hooting, yelling and shouting, were described as deafening even before the meeting began. The Chairman's opening remarks could barely be heard and when he asked 'Gentlemen, will you be quiet for a few minutes?', the concerted reply was 'No we won't!' The meeting became more boisterous as Police-Sergeant Smith mounted a form and demanded order, a command which was lost in a storm of whistling and hooting. By this time the hall was a seething mass of people, the entrance was blocked and many were in danger of being impelled down the stairs. Through all this, with admirable composure, Mr. Goff sat calmly smoking a cigarette. Some slight reduction in the volume of noise resulted from a call for quiet made by Mr. Edwin Martin of Ravine Hall, a prominent local Liberal, to the noisy elements, some of whom were presumably at least nominally, of his own persuasion. The candidate then spoke, or rather he shouted at the top of his voice and some at least were able to hear a little of what he said. However, as he concluded, a member of the audience rushed to the platform and made the suggestion that the meeting should be adjourned until Sunday when all the Ranters (Methodists) would be at chapel! Further calls from Mr. Martin for quiet went unheeded as the Hon. Mr Finch-Hatton, M P, began to speak. With remarkable aplomb he said how much he had enjoyed himself and to loud cheers congratulated his vociferous hearers on the intelligent interest they clearly took in politics. The Chairman then read a letter from Lord Salisbury but not a word could be heard. After a rather delayed Vote of Thanks from Mr. Goff to the Chairman, the meeting closed, but for many the proceedings continued in Murray Street for some time afterwards.

It has to be admitted that when addressing a meeting on the same evening in Hunmanby, Mr. Goff 'received a very cordial reception from a large and appreciative audience'. One wonders if this means that politics were taken more, or less, seriously in Hunmanby than in Filey.

A long standing custom in Filey was that fishermen supported the Liberal cause; at the time of the 1906 Election, the crew of a Filey yawl approaching Scarborough harbour, indicated their affiliation by flying a yellow flag. This caused some consternation amongst the local coastguards who used the International Code of Signals to identify the fishing boat as one carrying a case of yellow fever!

The local Liberal Party branch had, for many years, Club Rooms in Mitford Street; the building is now the St. John Ambulance Room. For the Conservative Party local branch a Constitutional Club built in Belle Vue Street to plans drawn up in 1897 is still a much appreciated social venue.

Filey was for many years in the Buckrose Division; in later years this became the Bridlington Division and in the mid-l980s, boundary changes brought the town into the Ryedale Constituency.

In the 20th century, Filey has been represented in Parliament by:

Mr. Angus Holden	(Liberal)
Sir Luke White	(Liberal)
Rear-Admiral Sir Guy Gaunt	(Conservative)
Major Sir Albert Braithwaite	(Conservative)
Mr. George Wadsworth	(Liberal)
Mr. Richard Wood	(Conservative)
Mr. John Townend	(Conservative)
Mr. John Spence	(Conservative)
Mrs. Elizabeth Shields	(Liberal)
Mr. John Greenway	(Conservative)

Elections, and in particular by-elections, are occasions when nationally known figures may be seen, if only fleetingly, in the town. One such was in February 1950 when a Labour Party meeting at the Conference Hall was so well attended that following it, the speaker, Lord Strabolgi, had to make his exit through a window. It is intriguing to speculate if he was a descendant of David de Strabolgi, sometime Earl of Athol, who in February 1332 was assigned land holdings in Fivele, (one of the many name variations of Filey).

Few party leaders have visited Filey. However in 1851 Punch included in one of its issues a cartoon of Lord John Russell, the Whig Prime Minister, on Filey beach. A memorable occasion for the town occurred in May 1986 during a by-election when at the Concert Hall, together on the platform, were two party leaders, the Rt. Hon. Dr. David Owen of the Social Democratic Party and the Rt. Hon. David Steel of the Liberal Party. Since that day the pattern of party politics has changed again and it seems unlikely that two party leaders will share a platform again either in Filey or elsewhere.

People

Every community has members who are talked about a little more or remembered a little longer than most. This may be because of the kind of person they were or because of the things they did, and Filey of course, had its fair share of those who may be included in these categories. Each one made his or her contribution and added to the social richness of the town. The relatively few we can today recall from memory, or know of from the written word, must be small in number compared with the many characters who lived out their lives here but of whom we now know nothing. The following few must serve to represent the many.

Visions of a past age may be created by the job description of Mr. Skinner who lived at Melton Cottage, near the Railway Station; he first entered Filey as a wheel postillion, an occupation he took up in 1835. On whose carriage he was riding at the time is not certain, but it may have been Sir William Millner's of Nun Appleton. Another familiar figure associated with wheeled transport in Filey was George Lowther, who, presumably for sheer enjoyment, drove his four-in-hand coach, the Rocket, between Scarborough and Bridlington, changing horses at the Royal Crescent Hotel, during the Season through the 1880s. He was the son and heir of Sir Charles Lowther Bt., of Wilton Castle.

Less affectionately remembered, although he wrote in 1853 an informative guide to Filey, and as a general practitioner had his admirers here, was Dr. Edward Pritchard. He had a medical practice in Rutland Terrace and his claim to fame (or infamy) was that in 1865 he was the last person to be publicly hanged in Scotland! The occasion attracted large crowds to Glasgow. His crime, committed after he left Filey, was to poison his wife and his mother-in-law.

A remarkable character who in later life took up residence in Queen Street overlooking the sea, was Albert Shakesby; his autobiography, published in 1923, and entitled 'From Street Arab to Evangelist', described his difficult early life in Hull, his conversion and his life both as a pugilist and as an evangelist. A man of exceptional strength which he employed in demonstrations of weight-lifting on the music-hall stage, his record in saving life in a variety of situations must have been almost unique. A generous man — some may remember him walking on occasion through Filey with a roll of tickets for a Saturday afternoon film show at the Grand Cinema; for a while Filey's streets would be witnesses to fast-moving young people anxious not to miss a free show.

A Filey man who refused to be overcome by circumstances was John William (Lorty) Jenkinson who, after losing an arm in 1900 at a Filey brickworks, became a sand artist, skilfully drawing pictures in the sand to be viewed by visitors walking along the Promenade. He also converted to a garden the steep bank at the end of Queen Street

It is difficult to resist making a comparison between the times taken to perform a noteworthy deed by the Watkinson family and Mr. Barker of the Three Tuns. Three generations of the first mentioned were responsible for 100 years of organ-blowing at St. Oswald's Church including most of the 19th century; Mr. Barker, however, in December 1869, took just a matter of a few seconds to realise that a lighted match was not the best source of light with which to look for a gas leak! Fortunately the resulting explosion at the inn was not a serious one.

A seaman who came to live in Filey and establish a family here was Charles Overy. He had previously survived one of the most feared experiences of the Arctic whalers — that of being trapped in the ice. The *Diana* left Hull in February 1866 for Greenland waters and by August the crew realised the vessel was unable to escape the ice floes. At times the crew members resorted to hauling the ship through cracks in the ice in their search for open waters, but by Christmas it was fully expected the vessel would be crushed Soon after, the shortage of food, the cold and scurvy had resulted in several deaths. Not until March did the *Diana* finally escape the ice, but with, however, an exhausted crew only seven of whom had not contracted scurvy. In later life Charles Overy was for several years Keeper of the Lifeboat House.

Residents of Filey at the turn of the Century were the Kendals. Mr. Kendal was an actor-manager well known on the London stage and his wife was Dame Madge Kendal celebrated for her Shakespearean roles; as sister of Forbes Robertson she was a member of a well-established theatrical family. 1896 was an important year for Mr. Kendal; he took the Garrick Theatre in the West End for the London Season and also bought The Lodge (now the White Lodge) as, during a visit to Filey, his wife had admired it. It was reported in the local press that her condition for agreeing to the purchase was that 'he would abstain from making her presents for a twelvemonth'. As it was also stated that Mr. Kendal's hobby was that of 'showering presents of costly jewellery upon his wife', we can only admire her wifely devotion. A lady with a somewhat imperious manner who, from her carriage, would on occasion summon shopkeepers from their premises, she was nevertheless a popular supporter of local charitable causes.

A resident remembered for somewhat different reasons was one who, at the onset of Winter, retired to his bed with a sack of monkey-nuts to hibernate until the arrival of Spring was confirmed. Perhaps he had better remain nameless.

Much missed still is John Morley, partner with his father at the blacksmith's forge in Mitford Street; his speech in pure Filey dialect was a joy to listen to. A story, which might even be true, records that when, early in their career, the Beatles arrived in Filey to stay at the Hylands Hotel (while performing in Scarborough), they asked John for directions to the hotel. Not knowing the identity of his enquirers, he explained to them that his refusal to help was because the management wouldn't let them in anyway.

Walter Gibson was another familiar Filey figure who was determined to earn a living in spite of great disability; with little use in his legs he tended from a sitting position his market garden near Muston Railway Crossing, and sold his produce from a pony-drawn cart during the 1950s.

Of the many local men who have done well in business, one is worthy of special mention. Dale Electric became a major maker of electricity generating systems with a world-wide reputation for quality and reliability. The founder was Leonard Dale who began his long career in electricity supply in 1935 by assisting in the wiring of new houses in the Filey area. Within months, at the age of nineteen, he established his own contracting business and then, twelve years later, the firm of Dale Electric (Yorkshire) Ltd. By the mid-1980s the business employed several hundred men and women and its annual turn-over had grown to over forty million pounds. The contribution made by the company to the local economy was a vital one.

Only limitations of space make it necessary to bring to an end this brief mention of some Filonians — and others; so many more there have been who are equally deserving of recollection.

CHAPTER SIX

Filey As A Holiday Resort

It is only in recent years that going away on holiday has become an experience enjoyed by the majority of the population. Difficulties of travel over anything but short distances discouraged the would-be traveller and until the 19th Century accommodation would leave much to be desired. Additionally, only members of the wealthier and more leisured classes could afford not to be at work. However, by the 18th Century there were enough such fortunate people to support the creation of spa towns around the country. Of this group Scarborough was soon a prominent and fashionable member and attracted many to take the waters, stroll on the beach and join the throng on the Spa.

By the early 19th Century, some visitors who found Scarborough a little too exciting began to appreciate the excellent beach and the relative quiet of Filey. About the same time, others realised that such a place had much to recommend it as a place in which to live. As early as 1806 a writer in the "Gentleman's Magazine" recommended Filey as a summer retreat to 'those who possess a relish for the pure exhibitions of nature, and take with them a little society'. The author also compared Filey favourably with the Firth of Edinburgh, the Bay of Naples and the Port of Constantinople.

By the 1820s transport to Filey from Scarborough was available by stagecoach. The Royal Union ran on Monday, Wednesday and Friday and the Original British Queen on Tuesday, Thursday and Saturday. There was also here a facility for anyone who wished to take a warm bath. Mr. Munro, referred to by Cole as 'Surgeon', possessed a portable tin bath which could either be lent out or used on Mr. Munro's premises. For those who were prepared to venture into the sea, Mr. William Hancote kept two bathing machines which were available for hire.

An early visitor to Filey was Lady Murray who in August 1822 arranged for the erection of a tent on Carr Naze close to the Spa. The reason for this was to enable her to entertain friends as they observed the Royal Yacht carrying King George IV on a visit to Edinburgh. It is likely that Filey's main street is named after her.

In these early years of the century accommodation for the visitor was provided at Mr. Thomas Foord's establishment known simply as The Hotel, at the Ship Inn, the Britannia and the Packhorse in Queen Street. Some lodgings 'on moderate terms' were also available.

In the 1830s Filey began to develop rapidly as a resort. Members of the long-established fishing community realised that visitors could provide a welcome addition to the sometimes uncertain income derived from fishing. This came from both providing accommodation in their homes and also making their boats available for pleasure trips. Taking visitors for a sail in the Bay later became known as 'spawing'. Newer residents who had recently built properties for themselves also began to appreciate the fact that there were those who were happy to pay handsomely for good furnished accommodation during the season. For these summer months some of the owners would take up residence in villages close to Filey.

By far the most significant development was Mr. Unett's New Filey estate bounded by The Crescent, West Avenue and North Street (later Belle Vue Street). The Crescent consisted of boarding and private houses, and an hotel, centrally placed. The hotel opened in 1854 with Edwin Taylor as lessee and it thus became known as Taylor's Hotel. It quickly acquired an enviable reputation for the quality of its accommodation and cuisine. It also soon became one of the centres of Filey's developing social life. A typical grand occasion was the Ball-Supper held on 13th July 1858, at which the dancing continued from 9 pm to midnight when the revellers were summoned to a 'sumptuous supper served in a most recherché style'. Afterwards the quadrilles, polkas, lancers and valses were enjoyed by the dancers until dawn. In February 1891, the diners at a social function at the hotel had some hard decisions to make in choosing from their menu:

Soup
Mock Turtle
Clear Oxtail
Fish
Turbot Soles
Removes
Sirloin Beef
Boiled Leg of Mutton
Boiled Turkey
Tongue
Roast Goose
Saddle of Mutton
Entremets
Plum Pudding
Pine Pastry
Tarts
Cheesecakes
Custards
Jellies

Blanc-Mange
Dutch Flummery
Lemon Sponge
Velvet Creams
Apple and Rhubarb Tarts
Swiss Pastry
Saronian Cream
Dessert
Pines, Grapes, Filberts, Oranges, Pears, Apples, Figs, Walnuts,
French Fruit, Almonds, Raisins, Tangerines, Pomegranates.
Plum Cakes, Ratafias and Biscuits.

    The growth of New Filey was rapid and, since the concept of a boarding-house built specifically to cater for summer visitors was such a new one to residents of Old Filey, almost all the boarding-house keepers were from other parts of the country. The census of 1861 indicates that all but a relatively few residents of Old Filey were born in the town but that almost all those now living in New Filey were from elsewhere. There was now, however, a great need for domestic help in the private houses, boarding-houses and hotels and much of this need was met by the girls and women who lived in or close to Queen Street. For those who found employment in the Crescent boarding-houses the hours were long and work was hard. Food would be prepared and cooked in the cellar kitchens (now often garden flats) and taken to the dining rooms overlooking the Crescent Gardens. 'Hot and cold in all rooms' was rarely applicable and carrying water for washing, up several flights of stairs, was a tiring part of the day's duties.

    Until well into the 20th Century almost all visitors to Filey would stay in a boarding-house, hotel or private house and would expect full board involving three meals each day. Those who took a furnished house would bring servants with them. There was little opportunity for 'eating out' except for one or two cafés providing light meals such as Albins at the corner of John Street and Murray Street, and Rowntree's Café (31-37 Rutland Street). The demand for accommodation at the height of the season was such that there were few parts of Filey where visitors could not find 'rooms'. Householders made temporary living arrangements for themselves in order to bring in a few extra pounds by 'taking visitors' and many lasting friendships were established in this way.

    Between the wars some Crescent boarding-houses were combined to form hotels. The Brigg, Ebor and Victoria Hotels were formed in this way as was the Hylands Hotel after World War II. Another type of accommodation was known as 'apartments'. This was similar to 'full board' except that the visitors would provide food which would then be prepared by the landlady. This could on occasions be very trying to the hostess who might be faced, at short notice, with the request to prepare for tea the results of an afternoon's boat fishing. The arrangement, very popular in the 1930s, had almost ceased by the 1960s.

In post-war years, the increasing number of facilities for eating out, the availability in shops of convenience foods and the preference for less formal holiday arrangements resulted in the conversion of boarding-houses and hotels to self-contained flats. Another relatively recent development is the ownership in Filey of a second or holiday home.

So in two centuries much has changed yet much remains the same. Filey's main attractions are still its gardens, the beach and the Brigg. Its centre is still compact with a wide range of goods for sale, though that range is a very different one from that available a century ago.

Informality is now seen to be the keynote in dress, catering and travel, and as a holiday venue, Filey now faces competition from inland centres and foreign resorts.

The Spa

Both of Filey's neighbour resorts have splendid spas which have contributed much to their popularity with holiday-makers and residents. Bridlington Spa is rightly widely known for its spacious Ballroom and comfortable Theatre. The Grand Hall at Scarborough Spa, recently refurbished, is one of the finest concert halls in the North of England. Filey Spa was never like either of these. It did, however, play its part in the development of Filey as a resort.

The Spa exists no longer. Its position on the north side of Carr Naze was idyllic on fine, warm, sunny days, but when a cold north-easterly wind blew, it would be only the most dedicated and determined seekers after health who remained long to take the waters.

Even during its most popular period in the late 19th century, it was no place for the faint-hearted. Situated close to the cliff edge, one or two steps in the wrong direction would have undone all the good that the waters might have achieved.

Its origins are unknown. Cole (1828) suggested that its medicinal virtues had been known for at least 150 years. If this is so, it must have been one of the earliest springs identified as having health-giving properties.

The Spa was an important facility for those visiting Filey for health reasons. An attendant was there during the season to dispense the water, and several small pavilions were built close by.

Many of the early 19th century claims for spa waters seem to us today to be exaggerated and dubious, and those for the waters of Filey Spa are no exception. Cole reports 'many most astonishing cures' and comments on the great reputation of the waters in cases of chronic rheumatism. Other disorders for which taking the waters was suggested to be efficacious included dyspepsia, hypochondriasis and nervous diseases generally, together with those of a scrophulous or scorbutic nature. The rate of flow must have been at one time quite substantial for suggestions were made about piping the water to a more convenient place. Perhaps this was partly because in the 1870s a dispute arose over the right of way to the Spa which was on privately-owned land. This contretemps resulted in the spring being boarded off. However, the water continued to flow to more accessible parts and a Victorian graffiti versifier inscribed on the boarding

"Though boarded up, It still flows out;
Drink for dyspepsy
Or for gout."

The Spa, like many others, gradually fell into disuse with the advent of more easily available proprietary medicines. The flow of water diminished and the site became more difficult to find. However, in 1951, as a project for Festival of Britain Year, members of the Filey Local History Group spent much time and effort in restoring the site. Erosion has since resulted in all remains slipping down the cliff into the sea.

The Crescent Gardens

A major factor in the successful development of New Filey was John Wilkes Unett's decision to designate a substantial area as pleasure grounds which subsequently became known as the North and South Crescent Gardens. For many years these gardens were for the enjoyment only of the owners and occupiers of, and visitors to, the houses on and close to The Crescent; in a manner similar to that which pertains today in some London squares.

The administration of the gardens was the responsibility of a Committee which first met at the Royal Hotel, Belle Vue Street, in February 1854 with John Clough as Chairman. The committee arranged the layout of the gardens and met the costs of upkeep by collecting subscriptions from those who were entitled to use the grounds. The committee remained in existence for 60 years during which time two of its major problems were ensuring that subscriptions were paid on time and making sure that unauthorised people were excluded. At the Annual Meeting in May 1887, it was agreed unanimously that someone should be employed to 'turn those lodgers out of the garden whose landlords do not subscribe'. As many of Filey's visitors at this time were people more accustomed to giving orders than receiving them, this resolution must have resulted in some heated exchanges.

In May 1893 another resolution prohibited the shaking of carpets and the drying of clothes in the gardens. At the same time, members agreed to purchase 12 notice tablets in order to discourage walking on the grass. An indication of

44. Filey Gardens in 1880.

changing times is seen in the decision in 1903 to admit anyone to the gardens on payment of 3d per day; a family ticket for four weeks could be purchased for 10s.

The link with John Wilkes Unett was maintained through the 60 years life of the committee. Mr. Unett was a member until his death in 1856. His son John became Chairman in 1859 and remained in office until 1876 when he was succeeded by Henry, John's son, who continued in the office of Chairman until the gardens were taken over by the Council.

In 1860 the decision was taken to engage a band to play in the gardens and the expenses incurred were met by subscriptions from visitors and residents. The subscription list was published week by week in the Filey Post. It would seem that the musicians played in the open as it was not until 1872 that the committee agreed to erect a Music Stand 'as soon as £100 is paid into the hands of the Treasurer'. With the Music Stand was built a 'commodious Summer House', but disaster struck on 5th November 1880 when the Summer House burned down. Clearly, the person responsible was known to the committee for he was threatened with legal proceedings if he did not forward to the members a 'nominal £10' as compensation.

From the late 19th to the early 20th century, children formed an increasingly large proportion of the visitors to Filey, and consequently a third image became associated with the gardens. Already established were the informal Church parade through the gardens following Sunday Morning Service and the stroll after hotel or boarding-house dinner. Both occasions were ones requiring the highest standards of dress. In Edwardian times there were now to be seen each day smartly uniformed children's nurses with their young charges. The Filey Post visitors' lists provide an excellent social comment on the times by indicating the perhaps surprisingly high percentage of families who were accompanied by nurses and governesses.

Through the 1920s and 1930s the gardens continued to be a vital and integral part of Filey's leisure facilities. A small orchestra played throughout the season and was listened to with pleasure and danced to with enthusiasm. A pre-war Filey Guide describes 'the strains of delightful music floating up from a sylvan setting', for the band-stand stood then where later was the Sun Lounge stage. Before the Sun Lounge was built there was a large area for open-air dancing. Was the weather better then or were we all a little hardier? In 1939 there was open-air dancing from 8 to 10.30 p.m. on Monday, Wednesday and Saturday to 'an orchestra of seven first class musicians'.

The outbreak of World War II brought music in the gardens to an abrupt end. On September 2nd the contract with R.M. Ackroyd and his Majors Orchestra was terminated and compensation of 17 guineas paid. In the following years the covered colonnade was partially enclosed by a barricade of sand bags whose condition deteriorated with time to leak liberal amounts of sand over the former dance area.

After the war, small orchestras were once again engaged to play in the bandstand for concerts and dances.

A major change occurred in 1961 when the decision to create a small concert hall was implemented. The colonnade was retained but not the bandstand. The name first applied to the hall was the 'Winter Gardens' but this was changed, shortly before the opening, to the 'Sun Lounge'.

Although the building had not escaped the problems often associated with large flat roofs, it proved a popular venue for a wide variety of social occasions.

Visitors

As it was designed to do, the development of New Filey, coupled with the arrival of the railway, led to a very rapid increase in the number of visitors. In days long before the creation of departments of tourism, T.V. advertising and the printing and wide distribution of coloured brochures, it must have been very much by word of mouth and personal recommendation that Filey so rapidly became known.

The middle years of the 19th century were also much previous to the days of holidays with pay, and thoughts of going away to stay at an hotel or boarding-house were held almost only by those of some substance. One significant difference between those days and more recent times is in the comparative numbers who came from different parts of the country. Today we know that a very high proportion of our visitors comes from West and South Yorkshire, the Midlands and the North-East; however, a century ago the pattern was somewhat different. A much higher proportion came from London and the Home Counties with relatively few visitors from the then West Riding.

What is quite understandable is that Filey was an obvious choice as a seaside resort for those families of means who lived relatively close by. Thus, the names appearing in the visitors' lists week by week included the Earl of Feversham's family from Duncombe Park, Helmsley, staying with Mrs. Barker at 24 Crescent in August 1873; Viscount Halifax and family from Pocklington staying at 3 Belle Vue with Mrs. Abbott late in the season in 1890, and Lord Londesborough at the Foord's Hotel in 1876. Sir Joseph and Lady Terry were frequent visitors in the 1890s, sometimes staying at Langford Villa, Lord and Lady Wenlock (Wenlock Place, Church Street presumably has a nominal link with the family) of Escrick Park, York, chose the Crescent Hotel in 1878 for their holiday as did Viscount and Viscountess Folkestone, who, in spite of their name, had only to travel from Nun Appleton, Tadcaster, in September 1872. The Howards from Castle Howard spent part of the summer at 26 Crescent in 1887, and from Burton Agnes Hall the Wickham-Boyntons took rooms with Mrs Webster on the Foreshore in the early Edwardian years. In the 1870s members of the Wombwell family of Newburgh Priory holidayed on the Crescent at numbers

15 and 17. Also choosing the Crescent in Edwardian times were Lord and Lady Bolton of Bolton Hall, Leyburn, who spent several weeks with Mrs Cunningham at No 2 and Lord Deramore's family from Heslington Park, York, who lodged with Miss Gibson at Osborne House. About the same time, at the same boarding house, Lord St Oswald's family came over from Nostell Priory for a July holiday The previous year they found accommodation with Mrs. Hall at 3 Melville Terrace.

One of the most splendidly situated summer residences was North Cliff Villa, and it was chosen in 1890 by the family of Lord Lascelles. In 1878 the family of the Archbishop of York took the house for the season and the Archbishop joined them when clerical duties allowed.

Another well-known churchman to visit Filey was Dean Farrar of Canterbury who stayed at Mrs. Dunn's Cliff Point Cottage in September 1888. One family which had only a short distance to travel in 1908 was that of Viscount Ennismore of Hackness Grange; Mrs. Cunningham's boarding-house at 2 Crescent, was their chosen holiday home. Lord and Lady Middleton had only a little further to travel to the Crescent Hotel from their home at Birdsall near Malton in October 1881; and Viscountess Helmsley of Nawton Tower would soon reach the Crescent Hotel in 1912 whether she chose to travel by road or rail.

For these visitors Filey would be one of the closest resorts to their homes and a popular choice, particularly for those who wished to avoid much travelling. However, the town clearly had its attractions for those who lived further away. In 1904 and 1905, young members of the Duke of Devonshire's family were staying at Mrs. Gibson's boarding house at 12 Crescent and in the closing months of the 1890s some of the Earl of Wharncliffe's family stayed at 37 Crescent. From Wentworth Woodhouse (reputed to be the largest private house in Britain), the Earl and Countess Fitzwilliam and members of their family came to stay on the Crescent over a period of several years choosing either the Crescent Hotel, 30 Crescent, or 2 South Cliff Villas. Viscount and Viscountess Mountgarret of Nidd Hall, spent part of the 1907 summer at the Royal Crescent Hotel and the following year their family stayed with Mrs. Whitfield at Glenavon on the Foreshore. From Kettering in 1902, 03 and 04, the Earl and Countess of Dalkeith, or members of their family, travelled to Filey to stay either at 2 or 3 Belle Vue. A family which made several visits to Filey between 1868 and 1888 was that of the Duke of St. Albans from Nottinghamshire. The Duke favoured the Crescent Hotel, but members of his family preferred either North Cliff Villa or Mrs. Haxby's establishment at 17 Crescent. In 1908 the Marchioness of Exeter brought her family from Burghley House, Stamford, to stay with Mrs. Barwick at 16 Crescent, but four years later she came alone to stay with Mrs. Cunningham at 2 Crescent. Perhaps near-neighbours Lord and Lady Cecil recommended Filey following their holiday at 11 Crescent in 1904 and 1905. A much earlier visitor from Stamford was Lord Kesteven who stayed at the Crescent Hotel in September 1878. Another Midlands visitor was Lord Byron (not the poet) who spent a holiday in August 1884 at the Spa Saloon (Ackworth). Also staying on the sea-front in August 1903, at Pitfour (now part of Southdown) were Viscount and Viscountess Combermere from Stafford. Regular visitors to Filey through the 1890s were family members of Viscount Newarks of Holme Pierrepoint. They usually chose Mrs. Atkinson's boarding-house at 19 Crescent.

The attractions of Filey must have been discussed over many of the Capital's dinner tables for week by week and year by year many made the long railway journey between London and Filey. Amongst these were, in 1874, Lord Loftus, and Baron and Baroness de Vaux and a little later, Viscountess Chewton (1878), also Viscount and Viscountess Tiverton (1908); Earl Waldegrave (1878); the Earl of Bessborough (1876); the Countess of Guilford (1908) and the Earl and Countess of Halsbury (1908). The Crescent Hotel was the popular destination for all of these visitors as it was also for other London residents, the Duke and Duchess of Newcastle (1890) and the Dowager Duchess of Northumberland in 1905. From Grosvenor Square in July 1881 Lord De Freyne also came to the Crescent Hotel and in August 1871 Lady Hamilton enjoyed the hotel's hospitality. The previous year, the Duke of Grafton's son, Lord Fred Fitzroy took the same route staying at both the hotel and 26 Crescent. In 1874, having a July seaside holiday there were members of the Duke of Westminster's family and those of the Marquis of Ely's. Wimbledon residents, the Earl and Countess of Chichester, had an autumn break in 1901. From Eaton Place to Varley's Crescent Hotel in September 1892, journeyed the Marquis of Ailesbury's son, Lord Brudenell Bruce and to the same hotel in July 1874, Baron and Lady Amphlett and party came from Wimpole Street. A later visit there was made by Viscount Hood in September 1909.

Others from London and the Home Counties staying elsewhere in Filey included the Earl and Countess of Verulam staying, in 1900, at 5 Unett Street (Southdene); the family of Viscountess Chelsea enjoying Mrs. Waggitt's hospitality at 28 Crescent; the Marchioness of Hastings from Windsor staying with Mrs. Bulmer on the Foreshore at Arndale in September 1906; members of the Marquis of Zetland's family, also on the front in 1912 at Mrs. Chapman's, St. Kitts; Lord and Lady Milnes Gaskill at Mrs. Cunningham's, 2 Crescent in August 1907; and the Earl and Countess of Yarmouth staying with Miss Preston at 27 Crescent. From St. James's Palace to Mrs. Proctor's boarding house at 31 Crescent in August 1907, came Lady Valda Machell, and to 15 Crescent in 1867-8-9, came members of a family with a rather fine combination of name and address — Lord Portman of Portman Square.

More distant travellers to Filey were Lord and Lady Alington and family from Dorset. Their chosen holiday home was 8 Crescent in August 1884. The Marchioness of Bath and family had a slightly shorter journey from Longleat to Mrs. Gofton's at 2 Belle Vue in 1899 and 1901. To 3 Belle Vue in 1908 came the Duke and Duchess of Norfolk and family from Arundel Castle; the family came again in 1910 and 1912. From Shillinglee Park, Sussex, in 1879, journeyed the Wintertons; the Earl staying at the Crescent Hotel, and the Countess and family with Mrs. Cullen at 15 Crescent. In August 1901, one of Mrs. Atkinson's guests at 19 Crescent was Viscount Torrington who had journeyed up to Filey from Kent. An earlier visitor from Kent was the Countess Stanhope who stayed with Mrs. Ellis at 1 Belle Vue in September 1892.

The rather difficult journey from North Wales did not deter Lord and Lady Penrhyn and members of their family who came from Penrhyn Castle, Bangor, to Filey several times between 1887 and 1905 to stay either at Downcliffe, the Ackworth, the Crescent Hotel or 3 Belle Vue; nor would Lord and Lady Decies have an easy journey from Windermere when they stayed with Mr. Cullen at 15 Crescent in June 1872.

Relatively few visitors came to Filey from the North of England or Scotland. Amongst the few were the Countess of Desart who travelled in September 1871 from Hexham to the Crescent Hotel; the family of the Earl of Mar and Kellie who stayed, in August 1901, with Mrs. Hall at 3 Melville Terrace; Lord and Lady Clive of Scothay Castle, Lanark, who chose the Crescent Hotel in 1871; the Earl of Northesk staying at the Royal Crescent Hotel in August 1900 and the family of the Earl and Countess of Minto from Hawick at Mrs. Railton's, 2 Melville Terrace in July 1893.

A family which became very closely associated with Filey over many years was that of the Earl and Countess of Ranfurly. The members made the journey many times between Dungannon, Ireland and the resort during the years 1884 to 1907, staying at the Crescent Hotel, 2 and 3 Crescent, and taking up residence often at Downcliffe. The Earl, who was appointed Governor-General of New Zealand in 1897, entered fully into Filey's social life, often acting as referee in sports and fishing competitions. Another visitor from Ireland was Lord Oxmantown who stayed in July 1909 at 12 Crescent.

Filey also achieved a degree of distinction as a holiday resort with several members of the European aristocracy for whom the Crescent Hotel was a popular place. These included, around the turn of the century, Count and Countess Telekei from Budapest; Count and Countess del Villar over from Madrid; Baron Massenbach and Baron and Baroness Von Shuralier of Darmstadt. Others staying about the same time were Baroness Van Langanan who came from Vienna to stay at Wave Crest; Count and Countess Kinsky lodging at 2 Belle Vue; Baroness de Chabonlan from Paris staying with Miss Shaw at 2 Rutland Street and Baron Lauer of Berlin on holiday with his family at Miss Preston's boarding house at 27 Crescent.

In August 1879, Count and Countess Karolyi took a break from diplomatic duties at the Austrian Embassy to enjoy the sea views from 16 Crescent. In 1909, Baroness Von Tubeuf preferred the more homely environment of 17 Church Street. One of Filey's very few Italian visitors was

Baron Rondi who in July 1879 was almost in the country while staying at Grove Villa on Scarborough Road. In August 1907 the Crescent Hotel entertained a guest from one of the most distant parts of the Empire in the person of the Ranie of Sarawak.

Filey was also popular with senior officers of the Army and Navy, from General Clarke of London in September 1877 on leave at the Crescent Hotel, to Rear Admiral Mosteyn Field staying with Miss Cappleman at Beach Haven in 1908. Other military men who found Filey a good place in which to enjoy a respite from duty included General Goddard of London staying with his family in September 1884 at Mrs. Hepton's boarding house at 4 Rutland Terrace; General Gloag and family enjoying Mrs. Scrivener's hospitality next door at number 3 at almost the same time; they perhaps recommended the establishment to General Cox of Guildford who took a summer break there in 1887.

The Crescent Hotel may have resembled a rather good officers' mess during one week in August 1890, when Colonels Goodchild, Beaumont, Collins and Pigott were staying there with their families. In 1896, General and Mrs. Philips chose Mrs. Atkinson's boarding house at 18 Crescent for their late summer break. 18 Crescent, was also popular with the Church, for staying there at various times between 1868 and 1909 were the Lord Bishop of Lincoln and family; the Lord Bishop of Wakefield and the Dean of Chester and family.

The visitors' lists produce some intriguing names; who were for instance, Mr. and Mrs Roosevelt of New York who spent a few days at 10 Crescent in August 1902? And how pleased would be the visitor to the Crescent Hotel in August 1896 who was listed simply as 'Hon. Trollop'? More familiar names are those of Sacheverell Sitwell, staying with his family at 18 Crescent in July 1874 and Mrs. C.F. Wedgwood from Burlaston at 15 Crescent in October 1871; Mr. and Mrs. A. Rowntree of York at 4 Parade (Foreshore) in July 1910; Mr. and Mrs James Reckitt, Hessle, at 11 Crescent in 1879. Mr. and Mrs. Barrow Cadbury, Birmingham, stayed at Mrs. Hall's, 27 Crescent, in August 1908; Master Neville Chamberlain at Mrs. Brown's, Belle Vue, in August 1881. Who was in the party brought for the season by the splendidly named Madame Risk Allah to Rose Cottage, Mitford Street, in 1876? In September 1905, one of Mrs. Cammish's guests at 6 Crescent, was particularly well-known in Yorkshire; he was the Hon. F.S. Jackson, Yorkshire's cricket captain.

Another notable family to visit was that of Titus Salt, the enlightened textile manufacturer who built the complex of mills together with the new town of Saltaire. In August 1871 he stayed at the Crescent Hotel while his son, Titus Salt, jnr. and family chose Mrs. Perryman's boarding house at 23 Crescent. In order to enjoy a break from civic duties in August 1910, the Lord Mayor and Lady Mayoress of London took up residence at the Royal Crescent Hotel.

A young visitor to Filey who later became internationally celebrated in the world of music was Frederick Delius. Born in January 1862 at Bradford, his father was a wool merchant who brought his family to Filey many times between

1876 and 1901. It was their practice to journey here from Bradford in a special carriage attached to a scheduled train. In later years Delius recalled with pleasure playing cricket in Gristhorpe and Hunmanby and spoke of a walk on the Brigg during which he was trapped by the tide. On August 19th 1879, while staying at Mrs. Colley's 5 Crescent, he played two violin solos, 'Cavatina' by Raff and 'Sonata' by Grieg, during a musical evening—perhaps one of the first occasions on which he played in public. Delius could not possibly have anticipated that just seven years later he would number Grieg as a friend while studying in Leipzig. Other houses at which the family stayed included 22 and 24 Crescent, Ivydale and Worlaby House in Rutland Street.

A visitor who later became equally well-known, but in the world of letters, was Charlotte Bronte, author of 'Jane Eyre' She came to Filey in June 1849, to rest following the distressing experience of being with her sister Anne at her death in Scarborough. Charlotte stayed for three weeks with her friend, Ellen Nussey, at Cliff House (now Brontë Café) in Belle Vue Street. Clearly she benefited by her stay for she returned in May 1852 to stay for a month at Cliff House; this time she was alone and walked often on the beach and bathed once in the sea. In a letter to Ellen Nussey she wrote '....I set out with intent to trudge to Filey Bridge (Brigg), but was frightened back by two cows. I mean to try again some morning.'

The Filey Post ceased publishing lists of visitors in 1915 and ceased publication altogether three years later. When World War I ended, England had changed so markedly in just a few years that it is unlikely that visitors would have been listed again even if the Post had continued publication. It perhaps seems strange to us today that readers apparently preferred to peruse long lists of visitors rather than additional items of local, national or international news. (The Scarborough Gazette contained, in high season, several large pages of visitors' lists). These lists do, however, enable us today to obtain a picture of holidaymakers at Filey in those far-off Victorian and Edwardian days.

The Royal Connection

Perhaps Filey's first royal visit was that made by Leopold II, King of the Belgians. It took place in mid-September 1873 during the King's voyage in his yacht to Scotland to stay with Queen Victoria at Holyroodhouse. At short notice he apparently decided to stay briefly in Scarborough for a private visit during which, in company with the Count D'Outremont, he drove over to Filey, alighting at the Crescent Hotel. From here they walked through the gardens and along the sands to the Brigg. Clearly it was a fine, early autumn day for on their return they sat in front of the Spa Saloon (Ackworth) to enjoy the view for almost an hour. They then returned to the Crescent Hotel just three hours late for luncheon which had been prepared for 2 pm.

A rather more prompt arrival for lunch at the same hotel was made seven years later by the Duke of Edinburgh, Queen Victoria's second son, known affectionately as the Sailor Prince. This was during an official visit by the Duke in his capacity as Admiral-Superintendent of Naval Reserves. He drove over in a coach and pair from Scarborough, accompanied by Commander Grant, the Superintendent of Naval Reserves for the Scarborough district, in order to inspect the Coastguard Station which then was at the seaward end of Queen Street. Here he was welcomed by a crowd of 200 including the several local coastguards in full uniform and fishermen in guernseys and sou'westers. After the inspection he was shown plans recently drawn up for a Filey Harbour scheme, and then, following lunch, left Filey in a special saloon carriage attached to the midday Hull train en route for another coastguard station inspection at Flamborough.

Almost ten years later the Duke of Edinburgh's nephew also enjoyed the hospitality of the same establishment. In August 1890, Prince Albert Victor, the elder son of Prince Edward (later Edward VII) drove from Scarborough in company with the Earl of Londesborough and Sir Charles Legard for a brief visit which included tea at the hotel.

Another of Queen Victoria's family to visit Filey was Princess Louise, the Queen's fourth daughter. She came over for the day from Harrogate in September 1899 with Lord and Lady Verulam, and in the afternoon spent half an hour shopping in the town.

Perhaps she recommended Filey to her niece Victoria, Queen Victoria's grand-daughter, for in 1900, Victoria and her husband Prince Louis of Battenberg, stayed for several weeks at 36 The Crescent with their children.

The Prince and Princess's children were — Alice (the mother of the Duke of Edinburgh); Louisa (later Queen of Sweden); George (later 2nd Marquess of Milford Haven) and Louis (later Earl Mountbatten). For the Prince, the time spent in Filey was a combination of business and pleasure. He was then Chief of the Naval Intelligence Department (he later became First Sea Lord of the Admiralty) and spent much of his time in local cobles investigating currents and tides. Louis, who was then just a few weeks old, contracted a childish ailment for which a remedy was supplied by local chemist W. Rickard. Clearly the medicine proved acceptable since, for several years afterwards, Mr. Rickard's advertisements carried the legend 'Under the patronage of Her Grand Ducal Highness, Princess Louis of Battenberg, Princess of Hesse'.

In June 1910, again perhaps as a result of a family recommendation, Ernest Ludwig, who was Queen Victoria's grandson (the Grand Duke of Hesse) stayed at The Crescent Hotel with his wife Eleanore and children George and Louis. (Louis was a popular family name). Ernest's younger sister, Alix, Tsarina of Russia, was assassinated in 1918.

A popular visitor to Filey in the 1930s was Princess Mary, the Princess Royal and daughter of King George V, who brought her sons George, later Earl of Harewood, and Gerald. The boys enjoyed early morning fishing trips with Thomas 'Tich' Jenkinson who provided them with an alarm clock with the recommendation that they should place it in a bucket in order to be ready to sail soon after dawn. The link was resumed in July 1955 when the Princess Royal presented Mr. Jenkinson with the B.E.M. for services to the fishing industry. The presentation took place in the open air when the Princess Royal was in Filey to open officially the Royal Parade.

In the following year, on May 16th, Countess Mountbatten, in her capacity of Superintendent-in-Chief, opened the local Divisional Headquarters in Mitford Street of the St. John Ambulance Brigade.

The Pierrots

In the closing years of the 19th century, visitors to the sea-side were beginning to expect entertainment of a rather less serious kind than the small orchestras and bands that had previously been the most usual music providers. Around the coast there were in the 1880s many troupes of Minstrels, but by the 1890s they were beginning to be replaced by the Pierrots in their equally distinctive costumes.

An early Pierrot — and one of the greatest showmen, was Will Catlin who first appeared at Scarborough in 1894 and eventually went on to develop the Futurist and Arcadia complex. One of the Pierrots in Catlin's Bridlington company was Ernest Taylor who adopted Andie Caine as a stage name. He came to Filey in 1895 and recognised that it was a resort in which he might establish his own troupe. Andie sang and played the banjo accompanied by George Fisher. They found it hard going at first and spent nights on the beach as the takings from their 'bottling' were insufficient to pay for lodgings. It must be added that their reception from some of the locals was less than cordial.

In August 1899 five pierrots, Teddy Myles, Charles Homer, Harry Collins, Edward Bleasdale and his brother Tommy were fined 40 shillings for performing on the Crescent. Tommy Bleasdale was unusual as a pierrot in that his chosen musical instrument was a harp.

However, by this time, Andie Caine's little band had become accepted and the performers were described as 'Royal Filey Pierrots' because, on occasion, members of the Battenberg family were in the audience. So began Andie Caine's association with Filey which was to last for 46 years until his death in 1941.

Not every visitor welcomed the pierrots; in 1903 the Council received a complaint that 'the town was being overrun by pierrots', that 'Filey was rapidly being brought down to the level of Margate and Yarmouth and that though Filey had been a haven of rest for the weary it was now like a moving, troubled sea.' These views were, however, only held by a small minority and Andie Caine's Pierrots established over many years great affection amongst residents and visitors. Children especially would know many comic routines by heart, but still ask for them to be repeated. The re-appearance, season by season, of favourite performers was eagerly anticipated by returning visitors. One such was the comedian Teddy Myles who was described in July 1903 as being 'in his eighth consecutive season, as light and clever and entertaining as heretofore'. Other later popular members were Carl Edwards — vocalist and entertainer, Fred Musson — comedian, Gus Yelrob and Billy Gill.

For many years the Royal Filey Pierrots became essential viewing for almost every visitor to Filey and Andie Caine became a respected and well-liked resident whose business interests were to include the Grand Cinema. He was also responsible for productions of London pantomimes and in 1910 these included 'Cinderella' at the Palace Theatre, Walthamstow, and 'Red Riding Hood' at the Palace, Tottenham.

The Pierrots performed during the day on the beach or the Foreshore and in later years at the Alfresco Pavilion behind the Royal Crescent Hotel on a site now occupied by Newton Court.

The hearing at Bridlington Police Court in 1906 when Andie Caine applied for a music licence for the Pavilion must have been nearly as enjoyable as a Pierrot performance for his demeanour was described as 'entertaining alike to bench, bar and the police'. It became something of a tradition for guests at the Crescent Hotel to stroll over to the Pavilion in evening dress after dinner and round off the day with an hour or more of music and laughter.

A Pierrot who came to and stayed in Filey was Lister Reekie. In his earlier days as an entertainer he had busked on Brighton Beach with Tom Walls who later made a very successful career in the theatre and in films and also achieved fame as the owner of a Derby winner, *April 5th*. On joining the Filey pierrot troupe in 1913, Lister Reekie was known as Cousin Punch; in the following year his benefit performance unfortunately coincided with the outbreak of World War I and the consequent exodus of visitors from Filey.

In 1931 he made an unexpected career change and established the Filey News; Filey's first local paper for many years.

Pierrots performed again in Filey on the beach and sea front soon after the Second World War, but somehow the magic had gone; perhaps with the increased popularity of the radio and gramophone audiences had become a little more sophisticated. Whatever the reason pierrots were a little later no more to be seen in Filey and an era of more than 50 years of popular light entertainment had drawn to a close.

Butlin's

No story of Filey would be complete without reference to Butlin's Camp. The association between Butlin's Ltd., and Filey extended from 1939

45. An aerial view of Butlin's Holiday Camp from the overhead cable system.

46. The outdoor pool at Butlin's.

over a period of 44 years and during that time the presence of the holiday camp had a considerable effect on the town.

The first definite indication that William Butlin was interested in building a camp close to Filey came in April 1939 when plans were submitted for approval to Filey Urban District Council. However, after discussion these were rejected on the grounds that such a development would represent 'a serious detriment to the neighbourhood' and that the buildings were 'out of keeping with the locality'. This response resulted in several changes to the plans being made and a special meeting being arranged between the Council, Mr. Butlin and the Manager of the Butlin's Camp at Clacton-on-Sea. The changes clearly were satisfactory for in May the amended plans were approved.

Work on the site soon began but just a few weeks later war broke out and a holiday by the sea was a concept soon to be distant from most people's minds. However, such a development, even in an unfinished state, could be used as a services establishment and it was taken over by the War Department. The Minister for War, Mr. Hore Belisha, then asked Mr. Butlin what he would charge to complete the camp and was given an estimate of £175 per occupant. This was a figure Butlin knew to be £75 less than the sum usually accepted by the War Department, but he coupled it with one condition; that at the war's end he would be able to buy back the camp at a price of £105 per unit of accommodation. This arrangement was readily accepted and construction went ahead. Almost the first major item to arrive on the site was the fountain from the Glasgow Exhibition which was delivered in September 1939. When eventually it was assembled in the boating lake it produced a circular pattern of illuminated water jets, and particularly on late summer evenings provided an impressive spectacle for campers leaving theatres and bars.

The initial function of the boating lake site was as a parade ground. When the camp changed in 1945 to its peacetime, civilian role some difficulty was experienced in submerging satisfactorily the slightly inclined parade ground; a situation which led to the then often heard comment that 'the tide was still out at Butlin's'.

In the early summer of 1945 half the camp was released by the War Department and the first holidaymakers began to arrive. The transition from war-time service station to peacetime holiday-camp was eased by the appointment by Mr. Butlin of Group Captain Ernest Borthwick-Clarke as the first Camp Controller; this new position required no change in place of employment for Mr. Borthwick-Clarke as he was previously Officer Commanding R.A.F. Hunmanby Moor, the name the camp was given as a service station.

After six years of war, campers came determined to have a memorable time and for many it was their first ever holiday away from home. To us today, their willingness to be organised into processions and group activities including physical training seems strange, perhaps it was partly due to the training received in the services which many had only recently left.

In order quickly to establish the name and reputation of the Filey Camp, Mr. Butlin arranged, in the Viennese Ballroom, a week of grand opera beginning on 21st October 1946 with a performance of La Boheme by the San Carlo Opera Company of Naples. The company, which came directly from Covent Garden, also presented later in the week the Barber of Seville, Cavalleria Rusticana and I Pagliacci. The following year on May 10th to celebrate the opening that day of the Railway Station by the Lord Lieutenant of the East Riding, Lord Middleton, and Sir Charles Newton, Chief General Manager of the L.N.E.R., a concert was given in the Viennese Ballroom. The soloist in Beethoven's Piano Concerto No.3 was Solomon accompanied by the London International Orchestra conducted by Anatole Fistoulari. These occasions were opened to local residents, a much appreciated gesture.

In those early post-war years holiday seasons were long; in 1947 the Camp opened on the 29th March and the last campers of the season departed on the 1st November.

In the succeeding years the camp grew in size and in the range of facilities offered. In the late 1950s at the height of the season 10,000 campers and 1500 staff would be together creating a holiday atmosphere which many found irresistible and to which they would return season by season. On arrival each camper received an enamel lapel badge indicating the year and the camp; some acquired a considerable collection of badges and wore as many as their lapels would hold.

Until self-catering facilities were offered in the 1960s all accommodation was in chalets of simple provision, and full board was available in the four Dining Halls of Kent, Gloucester, Windsor and York. Each camper was assigned to one of these and thus became a member of a House of that name. The intensity of the inter-house rivalry that was generated in games and competitions and exhibited by campers in their new found loyalties would supply a sociologist with material for a lengthy thesis. Children were particularly well catered for and evening chalet patrols allowed parents to enjoy evening entertainments during which they would glance occasionally at illuminated signs indicating where babies had been heard crying. The T.V. series 'Hi-de-Hi' conveys very well the atmosphere of the camp.

Several well-known entertainers began their careers at Filey; in the mid 1950s Charlie Drake was a boxing instructor and Des O'Connor, as a redcoat, did an excellent ad-lib act on a Saturday morning in the open air, sometimes in the rain, selling Butlin Church Reviews to campers waiting for coaches to take them home. A star by any standards was Big Charlie, an Indian male elephant weighing an estimated 8 tons. Transporting him from Ayr to Filey had been a major engineering challenge. He walked frequently round the Camp and was very popular with the holidaymakers. Sadly, when his mahout died he became difficult to handle and had to be put down.

Changing holiday patterns brought the introduction of self-catering facilities and campers indicated their increasing preference for less formal provision.

Although there had been indications in the early 1980s that all was not well with the Camp, it came as a considerable shock to the staff and to the town when in late 1983 it was announced that the Camp was to close completely. In the 39 seasons of the Camp's life a considerable number of jobs, both permanent and temporary, full and part-time had been taken by local people and would be sorely missed.

The average number of campers staying each season would be of the order of 100,000 and most of these would visit Filey at least once during their stay bringing much appreciated revenue. The many donations to local charitable causes made by Mr. Butlin (later Sir William) personally, or by the Camp staff, were always gratefully received.

So an era ended, the permanent staff dispersed and the local communities adjusted to the knowledge that no more would the Camp spring back into life with the beginning of another holiday season.

CHAPTER SEVEN

The Sea

Fishing

It is not possible to say for how long men have fished from Filey. It has been claimed that the origins of the Yorkshire coble are in the Viking long ship. If this is so then perhaps fishing was taking place here in the 9th century, and, if some of the earliest Filonians were fishermen (as seems likely), then it may be that fishing boats have launched from the beach over a period of 1200 years.

The earliest authentic references to the fishermen of Filey are to be found in church records. From a local history point of view it is fortunate that in the 12th century several disputes arose over the payment of tithes. In 1122 the canons of Bridlington Priory and the monks of Whitby Abbey disagreed; the Dean and Chapter of York to whom the dispute had been referred, decided that Whitby fishermen should pay tithes to Bridlington on fish landed by them at Filey, and Filey fishermen pay to the Abbey when landing at Whitby. This arrangement apparently did not always work well and in 1190, Hugh, Prior at Bridlington, complained of injustice as a result of which, in 1191, the dispute was referred to Rome. Pope Celestine III commissioned the Abbot of Rievaulx and the Priors of Kirkham and Warter to adjudicate. They instructed Whitby Abbey to claim tithes no longer from Filey fishermen. A few years later Bridlington was again successful in another similar dispute with the Prior of Grimsby.

These arguments about tithes of fish (a valued addition to the menu in any monastery) confirm that men from Filey were, in the 12th century, making long journeys by sail and oar to catch fish; though regrettably it is not possible to be sure of the design and size of the boats they were using. It is however, remarkable that the first dispute arose not very many years after William I had caused the district to be laid waste; a tribute surely to the powers of economic recovery of the inhabitants.

Although reliable records of succeeding centuries are scarce, it appears reasonable to believe that during this long period, there have always been Filey men making a living from the sea. In considering fishing through the ages, interesting questions arise. How was boat building financed in small, far from wealthy communities? How was the transport and distribution of fish organised? It is a matter of regret that there are so few records relating to fishing from Filey

47. Yawls were designed to sit securely on the sand; the crew of *Tranquillity*, skipper William Ross, clean the hull, about 1890.

48. This post-card was entitled 'Filey Fishwife'.
Unfortunately, her name is not given.

in earlier centuries. However, there is reference to a shipwright in Filey in 1501; no doubt he would be a builder of fishing boats. Certainly we know that as early as the 16th century local fishermen faced considerable competition from foreign boats. In 1560 it was reported that the Dutch fishing fleet on the English coast was several hundred strong. In 1603 Sir Walter Raleigh wrote a pamphlet to encourage fishing by Englishmen rather than Hollanders and Flemings. In 1635, Charles I received £30,000 from foreign fishermen for the right to fish on the English coast.

Tithes were an everpresent burden and two and a half centuries ago some of the tithe payers bore names which are familiar today; the names of Filey fishermen paying tithes between September 1731 and August 1732 included one Cammish (Thomas), two Rosses (Allan and Matthew), three Cappelmans (Peter, William and Nathaniel); the total number of tithe-payers being seventeen.

The larger fishing boats with which the Filey men would have been familiar had by the late 17th century evolved into single-keeled, three masted, decked, luggers with a crew of about five. They were sea-worthy vessels with, built into them, centuries of experience of North Sea vagaries of wind and tide. Further evolution in design took place resulting in the building, in July 1833 by Robert Skelton of Scarborough, of the first Yorkshire yawl; this was named the *Integrity*. It was 34 feet long and rather smaller than the so-called 5-man boats it was to replace. In the following two years several were built for Filey men. In 1872 the Filey fishing fleet included the following vessels and skippers:

Admiral Mitford	...	William Jenkinson
Admiral Hope	...	Castle Jenkinson
Refuge	...	Robert Jenkinson
George Peabody	...	Robert Jenkinson
Thomas and Mary	...	George Jenkinson
The Brothers	...	William Jenkinson
Emma	...	John Jenkinson
Monarch	...	John H. Jenkinson
Ebenezer	...	Richard Haxby
Felicity	...	Jenkinson Haxby
Concord	...	Richard Haxby
Unity	...	James Haxby
Diligence	...	Edmund Cammish
Sarah	...	Bayes Cowling
Eye of Providence	...	George Cowling
Jane and Elizabeth	...	Thomas Cowling
Rachel and Ann	...	Thomas Cowling
Zillah and Rachel	...	William Cappleman
Charity	...	William Crawford
Alpha	...	William Crawford
Indiana	...	John Crawford

49. Until the 1980s fish was auctioned on the Coble Landing.

50. Mending nets at the top of Church Hill.

51. Retired fishermen meet at the end of Queen Street.

52. Gathering shell-fish for bait from Filey Brigg and the rocks towards Scarborough was mainly the work of Filey's young and not so young women.

The Filey fishing fleet was at its maximum strength in the 1860s when there were reported to be 34 yawls worked by Filey men, in addition to 17 herring cobles and 64 inshore cobles. Each yawl of up to 40 tonnes displacement had a crew of 6; skipper, mate, 2 sharemen and 2 boys. Each herring coble required a crew of 4, and an inshore coble a crew of 3.

Local fishing followed a year round pattern; from early February to early June the yawls would be used to line-fish mainly for cod, halibut and haddock. Then there would be a change to net fishing for herring as the shoals migrated down the coast. The boats usually followed as far as Great Yarmouth; in 1812 eight Filey 5-man boats are recorded as going there. The yawls used Scarborough as a main harbour, but would sometimes land fish at Filey by anchoring in the Bay and transferring the fish to a small boat; they could also anchor inshore and beach as the tide receded.

The large herring cobles would also join in herring fishing and the inshore cobles would fish through the winter when conditions allowed. In 1789, perhaps surprisingly, the two fishing stations on the Yorkshire coast with the greatest numbers of first class, that is large, vessels, were Filey and Staithes; Filey having seven and Staithes nine. The larger communities of Whitby, Scarborough and Bridlington concentrated on maritime trading. In 1815 Bridlington relied on Filey for much of the fish it required. The Filey men did however depend very much on the harbour facilities the larger towns possessed. Although most of the fish caught on the Yorkshire coast was consumed in the North of England, some went much further afield; in the 18th century a considerable quantity of dried and cured fish went to northern Spain. Local techniques involved the split and salted fish being spread out to dry, then being allowed to stand in a pile for several days after which the fish were again exposed to the elements. The Filey curers acquired a reputation for drying skate to the consistency of horn.

The Napoleonic Wars had three effects on local fishing. The export of dried fish to Southern European markets was very seriously affected; the expansion of the Royal Navy increased the activities of press-gangs on the Yorkshire coast, putting at risk local fishermen in spite of some dispensations being made by which they were supposedly exempted; and a hazard to all shipping on the coast was the appearance in local waters of French privateers. In 1794, fishing on the Dogger Bank was seriously disrupted by the activities of these foreign raiders. Later in the same year there came an opportunity for a little local retribution. A British brig carrying corn had been captured by the French and manned by a prize crew. However, while taking shelter from a storm in Filey Bay the prize crew was overwhelmed by Filey fishermen and the vessel regained. In August 1797 a battle-royal took place off Filey when a Scarborough five-man fishing boat with its crew augmented and armed, chased a French privateer with four guns and a 20-strong crew. After a fierce encounter the enemy vessel was captured and taken to Scarborough.

To launch a coble from the beach, or to bring it out of the water using three horses, was a skilled operation, especially when there were breakers of any size. It required horsemanship of a high order to control horses in the sea, for them a far from natural environment. It was necessary for men to stand, sometimes waist deep in the water and lift, with their backs, the boat off or on to its carriage. In order to synchronise their lifting, the launchers joined in a form of rhythmic chanting of a form seldom heard today in any occupation.

Horses were replaced by tractors in the early 1950s. Although this modern form of traction requires skilful handling at the water's edge, and moving boats in this way through the surf has its own fascination, the sight on Filey sands of experienced men and horses working together was unsurpassed.

Fishing has always been an occupation requiring skill and strength, particularly in the days before the introduction of motors. The then preferred means of propulsion was sail-power but in the absence of wind, oars would be used. A pull of several miles in a coble would sometimes be necessary, and a yawl becalmed off-shore would be towed back to port and the fish market by some of the crew rowing the small boat carried by the yawl.

For Filey men sailing out of Scarborough the week would frequently begin with the journey there by the first train on Monday, each man carrying with him much of his food for the week. Even after the advent of the railway, for some, Scarborough would be reached on foot. After a week's fishing, perhaps on the Dogger Bank, the yawls would return to port in time for the men to be at home for the week-end.

In few occupations were the men so dependent on the women of their family as they were in fishing. Baiting fishing lines was frequently done by wives, daughters, mothers, aunts. However, whereas today mussels are delivered almost to the doorstep, in earlier times many of the women and girls would scour the rocks both north and south of Scarborough for flithers (limpets). Sometimes they would use a rope to reach otherwise inaccessible rocks. A successful search would often mean carrying the flithers in a maund (basket) during a long and tiring walk back, for the rail fare to and from Scarborough could not always be afforded. Next would come hours in the baiting shed attaching the bait to the hooks and coiling the lines in preparation for them to be carried, perhaps by a yoke across the shoulders, to the coble landing. Housework had to be fitted in with these duties and for some, if there were spare hours, they would be used in knitting guernseys. Life was hard for both men and women, and for children the few short years at school were soon over and both boys and girls would enter the world of work almost before they entered their teens.

Fishing was always one of the most hazardous of occupations Local weather lore was based on long experience, but deteriorating weather conditions could not always be foreseen. Yawl crews might find it necessary to run before the wind if caught far out in the North Sea and coble fishermen caught behind the Brigg in the rapid onset of gale conditions required courage, skill and

53. Bringing boats ashore with horses was always a skilful operation; this particular recovery took place in the 1950s.

strength to return safely to shore. Many fishermen have been lost in the broken water close to the end of the Brigg.

Long remembered on the East Coast was the storm of October 1869. Of the experiences of the Filey fishermen we have some knowledge from the splendidly titled and sub-titled 'God's Hand In The Storm; being a narrative of the Perils, Losses, Prayers, Deliverances Etc. of the Filey Fishermen in the Gales of October 1869'. This short work by the Rev. G. Kendall of Filey sold 4,000 copies of its first edition and subsequently ran to a second edition.

Thirty-one Filey yawls sailed from Scarborough on the fine Autumnal morning of Monday, October 25th. As they reached the fishing grounds thirty miles off, the wind rose and soon reached gale force; the storm persisted through Tuesday, Wednesday and Thursday without abating. The fishermen, who had put to sea anticipating a profitable week's fishing, soon found themselves in a desperate struggle for survival. Richard Haxby senior, skipper of the yawl *Unity* saw the Scarborough boat *John Wesley* sink with the loss of all the crew and was powerless to help. Some time later when there was no more to be done on deck he gave instructions for himself to be lashed to the tiller and ordered the other members of the crew below where there would be less danger. John Ross on the *Charity* reported how a wave washed away the yawl's coble. Richard Haxby junior and his crew of the *Ebenezer* expected to go down within minutes when they were struck by a powered vessel; they were amazed and much relieved to find their vessel had not sprung a leak. When the members of the crew of the *Felicity* had done all they could to secure the ship they joined in a short service led by the skipper, Jenkinson Haxby, a respected member of Ebenezer Chapel. After three days of tempestuous seas, George Jenkinson stood on the deck of *The Good Intent* and called into the wind, "Where is the God of Elijah?" He testified how the response gave him faith that they would survive the storm.

Families and friends waiting anxiously on shore slept little, sent off telegrams to ports up and down the coast and, in hope, were at the station to meet every train. The rejoicing when finally every Filey man was safely accounted for can be imagined; that not one crew member of the 31 Filey yawls had been lost was regarded as miraculous.

A particular risk for yawl fishermen was to be caught in a sudden squall while working lines from the coble carried by a yawl. This happened to M. Scotter, W. Jenkinson and J. Cappleman when 30 miles from land in February 1876. The coble was overturned by a huge wave and the men were thrown into the sea. The yawl was the *Elizabeth and Susannah* and only by outstanding efforts were the skipper, Matthew Jenkinson and the other yawl crew members able to effect a rescue of the three fishermen. Regrettably, the list of Filey men known to have been lost at sea is a long one, and certainly the number lost whose names are unrecorded would comprise an even longer list. In their excellent book, Irene Allen and Andrew Todd refer to seventeen men of the

54. Cork life-jackets were clearly not comfortable to wear.

Jenkinson family who were drowned while fishing and whose names are on memorial stones in the churchyard.

The losing of a single life at sea is tragic, but often there was a particular degree of sadness in losses involving small fishing boats as so often the crew members would be close relatives or friends. An example of this was the loss in October 1908 near Ravenscar of Richard Overy of Queen Street who, while crewing the herring coble *Harriet,* was drowned in spite of the efforts to save him of his father who was the skipper, his eldest brother, brother-in-law and nephew.

An indication of the cohesion of the Filey fishing community was to be seen when the funeral of a member took place. The loss of one of a close-knit, inter-related body of people was deeply felt as shown by the account of a funeral procession in 1908:

> 'Looking in the direction from which the music came, which was towards the old town, I saw a solid mass of people coming at a foot pace down the slope towards the other end of the bridge from where I stood. In front was a group of thirty or forty fishermen, four abreast, all in their spotless, dark blue knitted jerseys, all slowly stepping on, and all joining in Dr. Watt's well-known hymn,
> "There's a land of pure delight."
> They were singing with a solemnity and feeling, and a faith in the reality of the sentiments of the hymn, that shone out from their bronzed, uplifted, and ecstatic faces, more strikingly than words can express. For these men there was a settled peace and a religious confidence that the storms of modern theological criticism passed over and left as unshaken as their own Filey Brigg in the lapping of summer waves. Behind them the coffin, with one or two wreaths of flowers upon it, was carried by six stalwart brother toilers of the deep, and it was followed by the widow and the more distant relatives of the deceased, while closing the procession came the wives and sisters of the fishermen, and other sympathising friends. Onwards the slowly stepping funeral group came, under the over-arching green trees, through patches of sunshine and shade, still singing the hymn, and past a few bare-headed spectators, until it entered the ancient church'.

Bearing in mind the ever-present hazards of fishing, it is remarkable that, in October 1863, John Jenkinson and William Jenkinson were able to speak of their 63 years and 70 years respectively experience of the sea. The occasion was the gathering of evidence at Filey by James Caird, M.P., and Professor T.H. Huxley, F.R.S. into the effect of the introduction of trawling on East Coast fishing. (Professor Huxley was the scientist who defended Charles Darwin

55. Veteran Filey fisherman Healand Sayers is the raconteur in this photograph eminiscent perhaps of the celebrated picture 'The Boyhood of Raleigh'.

during the furore created by the theories of evolution contained in Darwin's book 'The Origin of Species').

War-time added another danger to an already hazardous occupation. Mines constituted a particularly insidious peril and claimed many lives. Submarines operated very close to the coast, particularly in World War I. The *Susie* was the last yawl to fish out of Scarborough and on the night of August 17th 1917, the skipper, Mark Scotter and crew — Reuben Scotter, John William Jenkinson, Matthew Wright and Tom Williamson, were fishing off Scarborough. Reuben, John and Matthew were in the coble working the fishing lines when a German submarine surfaced and fired on the yawl, killing the skipper. Before the yawl sank, the crew lifted his body into the small boat and rowed through the night reaching Scarborough about seven in the morning.

Just three months earlier a strange episode also involved a German submarine. After first taking the crew on board, the U-boat sank the herring coble *Edith Cavell*. The commander, who was clearly more humane than many of his kind, released the coblemen, George William (Chewy) Hunter, skipper; William (Stringer) Cammish, mate; Richard (Dicko) Johnson, Jack (Jacky T) Cammish, and George (Young Chewy) Hunter to a neutral Swedish vessel off the Farne Islands and they finally arrived back in Filey by train.

The effective marketing of fish sometimes presented nearly as many problems as its catching. The very short period of time that elapses between the taking on board of fish and its becoming unsaleable unless frozen or dried presents the greatest challenge. Local communities could of course be relatively easily supplied by Filey men, with much going to Scarborough and Bridlington. Before the building of the Hull to Scarborough railway line, transporting fish further afield was difficult because of the poor state of the roads. However, as early as 1842, four years before the railway reached Filey, it was possible to buy fresh Filey fish in Manchester. This was achieved by conveying the fish landed in Filey to Hull by cart in time to catch an early morning train to Manchester. The Flamborough and Filey Bay Fishing Company opened a shop in the city with fish on sale which had been out of the water less than 24 hours.

The completion of the Hull to Scarborough railway line made it much easier for fish to be transported quickly to all parts of the country and often fish wagons were attached to passenger trains to reduce journey times. This practice still continued after the introduction of diesel multiple units in the late 1950s. The gradual introduction of refrigerated lorries resulted in a steady decrease in the amount of fish transported by rail from Filey.

After World War I only coble-caught fish was landed at Filey, but the total weight could be considerable and the auctioning of fish on the Coble Landing continued into the 1950s.

In spite of the many problems, both natural and man-made, faced by local fishermen in recent years, the profession is still followed by some Filey men and fishing continues to make a major contribution to the local economy. It

56. A Filey Yawl in Scarborough Harbour with Mark Scotter (skipper), Matthew Wright, William Cammish, George Cammish, John William Jenkinson and Reuben Scotter.

57. Cobles on shore and yawls in the Bay create a busy scene about 1900.

is profoundly to be hoped that those nations which border the North Sea attain soon a sufficiently high degree of maturity to enable them to care properly for its waters and its living resources.

The Lifeboat Service

The sea-farer's life has always been one which has contained a strong element of danger. Even today accidents occur even though almost all vessels are powered and even quite small boats carry electronic aids to navigation and radios by which assistance may be summoned. How much more dangerous life at sea was, when propulsion was by sail or oar and when navigational aids were of the simplest, can be appreciated by reference to 'the Wreck Register For 1872-80'. This records that, around the British Isles, the number of wrecks in 1880 was 2,519. This appalling toll brought the total for the years 1855-1880 to 51,841 shipwrecks with a loss of 18,550 lives. One would imagine that in human life and in economic terms the cost would hardly be sustainable, yet men still continued to go to sea impelled often by love of the sea, but frequently from sheer economic necessity. Sadly, the vessels themselves were, in numerous cases, unworthy of the men who sailed them. In the days before the introduction of safety regulations and requirements like the Plimsoll line, ships were often sent to sea by unscrupulous owners, agents and charterers in an unseaworthy condition.

Another factor which added to the inherent dangers already mentioned was the rapidity with which the weather could change and the uncertainties which were almost always present when attempts were made to predict the weather.

If the history of sea-faring is besmirched by those who sent men to sea in unsafe vessels, it is honoured by those who, as willingly, risked life and limb in efforts to save those in peril. Until the early 19th Century the establishment of lifeboat stations was as a result of local endeavour, for the R.N.L.I. did not come into being until 1824.

The continual loss of life at sea as a result of stress of storm was a matter of increasing local concern and in 1823, Thomas Hinderwell, the author and historian of Scarborough, opened a fund with the intention of establishing a lifeboat station at Filey. Contributions were soon received partly as a result of the letters he wrote to York and Hull newspapers and a lifeboat was built by Robert Skelton of Scarborough. The boat was housed on the Foreshore near Carrgate Hill. Apparently no name was given to this first lifeboat and unfortunately there are few records of the rescues it effected.

The Filey Life-Boat Station was taken over by the R.N.L.I. in 1852 or 1853, and in 1863 the Station received its first boat to carry a name. It was *Hollon,* named in honour of a great benefactor of the Institution, R.W. Hollon of York. It was replaced 21 years later by *Hollon II,* which itself was succeeded in

1907 after 23 years service by *Hollon III*. These three vessels were credited with saving 169 lives in a total of 74 years service.

In 1937, the *Masterman Hardy* arrived on station but was to serve only 3 years before it was replaced by the first motor-vessel to be stationed at Filey, *The Cuttle,* so named because it was presented by Mrs. Florence Cuttle of Rotherham. In 13 years of service it was involved in saving 28 lives. It is perhaps surprising that it was not until 1940 that a powered vessel was first employed here. 1953 saw *The Cuttle* replaced by *Isa and Penrhyn Milstead,* which was at Filey until 1968 when the *Robert and Dorothy Hardcastle* took up station. Tuesday, 21st May 1991 was a great day in Filey's recent history; the *Robert & Dorothy Hardcastle* sailed out into the Bay to welcome the *Keep Fit Association*, Filey's new 'Mersey' class lifeboat; on shore were 3,000 residents and visitors to add to the welcome.

To be coxswain of a lifeboat is an honour in a community where standards of seamanship are high. It is of the greatest importance that the crew members have complete confidence in the one who may, on occasion, have to make rapid decisions in situations of great potential danger. It is a matter of regret that records do not reveal the names of the early coxswains. Thomas Jenkinson who retired in 1881 is the first whose name we know. His successor, Crompton (Crump) Wyvill served for 13 years, a length of service equalled by the next cox, George (Ding I) Scales who retired in 1907. For the next 8 years the coxswain was a well-known Filey character and respected seaman, Matthew (Brazzie) Jenkinson, and he was followed by Richard Cammish (Dicky Hoy) Jenkinson who held the position for the remarkable span of 20 years. Following his retirement, Thomas (Boysher) Cappleman served for 12 years until 1947. The next appointment was that of William Robinson who remained in charge until his retirement in 1963, when William (Dag) Chapman was appointed. Next to serve as cox'n was Thomas (Eamon) Jenkinson who began his period of office in January 1967 and continued until 1981 when he was succeeded by his brother Frank. The next change in office occurred in 1988 when Graham Taylor was appointed, who thus combined the positions of engineer and coxswain until 1998 when he retired to be succeeded by Malcolm Johnson who served for five years. The present holder of this very responsible position is Barry Robson.

The story of the Filey lifeboats contains many stories of dangers faced with heroism, dramatic rescues effected and the willingness of crews to turn out in all weathers and sea conditions when a need was perceived. The excellent book 'Golf, Lima, Foxtrot, Echo', whose title refers to the lifeboat's international call sign, describes some of these occasions and the author, Jeff Morris, gives a very informative account of the story of Filey's lifeboat station from its inception until 1976. The story is continued by the same author to 1991 in his book, *The Story of the Filey Lifeboats*.

Launching the lifeboat with horses was always a difficult operation and could sometimes be dangerous, as was indicated in January 1912 after the news was brought that a trawler was aground under Speeton Cliffs. In thick fog and strong surf the boat was being brought into the water when a carriage wheel sank in a pocket of soft sand. One horse was thrown down and the boat, with the crew on board, almost capsized. The crew members and launchers ('skeeters') were almost engulfed by the waves but the situation was saved by men on the beach hauling round by rope the lifeboat's stern so that the bow faced sea-wards. The crew was thus able to row out from the surf.

The following day eleven cobles were caught in a heavy northerly swell behind the Brigg; waves on the Brigg were reported to be breaking up to 40 feet high. The lifeboat was launched, but as most of the regular crew were already at sea the number was made up by retired men who enabled the lifeboat to escort the cobles to safety. The men would no doubt be remembering that just two days previously, Richard Johnson had been washed overboard from a coble and saved from drowning only by the skilful boat-handling of the other crew members.

How valued today would be first-hand recorded accounts of some of the oared lifeboat rescues. One such occasion was in December 1909 when the Hull steam trawler *Pelican* went aground in thick fog and stormy seas under the precipitous Bempton Cliffs. Both *Hollon III* and the Flamborough lifeboat *Forester* reached the vessel and in the rescue all nine members of the crew, who had climbed the rigging to escape the waves, were taken off by breeches buoy in pre-dawn darkness.

One of the Century's worst storms occurred in February 1871. In such weather the waters off Flamborough Head were particularly hazardous for sailing vessels as the crew of the North Shields schooner *Mary* were to find. Dismasted while off the headland the vessel was observed in Filey Bay drifting towards Filey Brigg. The *Hollon* was launched from the beach close to the Brigg and in the face of strong winds and mountainous seas battled its way to the ship and effected the rescue of all the members of the crew just minutes before the ship struck the rocks, broke up and sank.

Such brief, factual accounts convey little of the elements of danger, noise of storm, fine seamanship and skilful use of rescue equipment, all of which must have been present on these and many other such occasions.

The replacement of sail by engine for propulsion of commercial shipping has not ended calls for lifeboat assistance from coastwise vessels. Seamanship of the highest order was required by the lifeboat crew in December 1983 in rescuing the crew of the coaster *Rito* which was listing badly in heavy seas near the Brigg. Fourteen approaches to the vessel were necessary before all members of the ship's crew were finally saved. All the lifeboatmen received well-deserved awards for their services in this rescue.

Lifeboat Day in Filey was an increasingly important occasion; known at the turn of the Century as the Lifeboat Annual Demonstration, the order of events would then be typically for six horses owned by George Colling to draw the boat around the town with the crew aboard wearing their red caps and cork

58. Lifeboat Day about 1905; the Filey Band waits to follow the lifeboat into Mitford Street as pierrots collect from onlookers.

life-belts and with Filey Brass Band preceding the boat. In addition to making contributions to collectors with boxes, visitors and residents would throw coins into the lifeboat as it processed through the streets. A launch and manoeuvres at sea completed the demonstration. In 1903 the collection totalled £21-15s-0d. In recent years, Lifeboat Day has sometimes included spectacular aerial displays in addition to demonstrations of co-operation between lifeboat and helicopter.

On occasion, the lifeboat crew would take part in fund-raising in inland towns and cities. In July 1896 the crew journeyed to Leeds for Lifeboat Day there, appearing at the City Varieties, the Grand Theatre and the Theatre Royal.

An important Unit which operated from cliff or shore often in association with the lifeboat, was the Volunteer Life Saving Rocket Brigade. One of its functions was to project a line across a vessel which had gone aground and use it to carry seamen to safety by means of a breeches buoy. If the Brigade could get close to the ship a lead-line would be thrown and on training exercises lead-line heaving competitions were held. William Cunningham, Alf Long, or Ed. Sharpe usually did well in pre-World War I days with throws of about 30 yards. An occasion when the Brigade was of inestimable value took place in February 1900; the Hull steam trawler *British Empire* was aground under Speeton cliffs but Captain W.G. Long and other members placed a line by rocket across the vessel and saved all sixteen members of the crew. In November 1907 Captain Long's forty years service as rocket-firer was recognised at a dinner at the Imperial Hotel. (The character actor, A.E. Matthews, was Captain Long's nephew).

There is now much less need for the kind of apparatus which was so valuable in sailing-ship days. However when occasion demands the Coastguard Service has in its ranks local Auxiliaries who are trained and experienced in cliff rescue.

Changes in life-saving requirements at sea, and the development of light and fast boats, brought to Filey in 1966 an inshore life-boat (I.L.B.). This craft and its successors have since been invaluable on many occasions and the crew members have achieved an envied reputation for the speed with which they can react to an emergency in the Bay or on the Brigg.

In the years since a lifeboat was first stationed at Filey, shipping on the East Coast has both diminished significantly in volume and radically changed in nature; however, going on the sea for pleasure, an activity almost unheard of in 1823, now results in many call-outs for the lifeboat crews.

Filey continues to take pride in both its lifeboats and the men who crew them, and enthusiastically supports them in their invaluable service.

Shipping

Although Filey has never had a harbour, it has had direct and indirect connections with shipping over a very long period. However, little can be said with certainty about the vessels using Filey beach during the centuries before the Norman Conquest, and we can therefore only surmise about the ships that early inhabitants of Filey saw as they gazed out to sea. We do know that many vessels of past years were designed to land on sandy beaches similar to that at Filey, and other vessels could anchor in the Bay and load and discharge cargo or, embark and disembark passengers by means of small boats. Goods and people could therefore be moved in and out of Filey Bay legally or illegally. Reference in 13th century records to the 'Port of Filey' is one confirmation that this did occur in Medieval times. A little later, in 1324, it was reported that the Port of Filey, amongst many others, was to be watched in order to prevent John de Stratford from leaving the country. He had been found out in the risky enterprise of swindling Edward II. In 1364, during war with France, John Page of Filey was one of many who were empowered to detain any one attempting to leave the country without the King's special licence.

The Lord of the Manor was entitled to a local duty when goods moved through Filey and in 1600 the Lord of the Lennox manor claimed as 'groundage', 6d. for ships using Filey. The sea was, of course, the means by which Filey could be used as an entry port for coal from the North-East coalfields and the manor lord expected to receive two bushels of coal from each collier landing here. The transporting of coal through Filey was carried on until the late 19th century; 65 cargoes of coal were brought in during the years 1839 and 1840 and dues were paid on 68 cargoes of coal or timber in the period 1884-89.

Medieval Filey could be described as a mixed economy community as it depended almost entirely on both fishing and farming for its economic health. There were occasions, however, when almost without warning, a welcome addition might add, for a while, to the material well-being of the inhabitants. Such an occasion seemed initially to have occurred in 1258 when, as a result of a shipwreck close by, two sailors who survived the wreck sold to locals a quantity of goods from the ship. This transaction contravened the then Maritime Law, and King Henry III appointed Peter de Percy to investigate. As a result, the goods were confiscated, leaving the local inhabitants worse off — unless they were sufficiently devious not to have revealed all their purchases.

Some years later, in 1311, another local wreck gave up a chest of gold florentines and silver worth then £300, treasure indeed. However, this time the ship belonged to King Edward II who instituted an enquiry to find out what Robert de Lacey had done with this valuable cargo.

No queries resulted from a wreck on Hunmanby sands seven years later; ropes and masts to the value of 40 shillings were legitimately claimed by the Lord of the Manor.

1344 saw another vessel ashore near Filey while on passage from Scotland to London. Again, no time was lost in taking advantage of this windfall and it was reported that 30 Filonians, including one knight, carried away the cargo. Hauls like this must have been warmly welcomed by a small community existing on a survival economy.

One Maritime Law which must many times have faced coastal communities with a real dilemma was this; if a vessel became a wreck nothing could be legally taken from it if there were survivors. What wrestling with conscience there must have been for impoverished watchers observing a laden vessel in distress with crew members who might, with assistance from the shore, be saved. In 1542 the *Martin,* on passage from Aberdeen to Dieppe, was wrecked near Filey Brigg. Local people helped themselves to everything of value in the ship totalling £600. James V of Scotland protested vehemently about this since there had been three survivors.

On the 16th August 1561, locals looking out to sea, and fishermen off-shore, may have been intrigued by the sight of a large fleet making slow progress northwards across Filey Bay. Fifty-two smaller vessels were escorting two large galleys, one of which was white and the other had a flag on which was emblazoned a gold and blue fleur-de-lys.

What was this fleet and whither was it bound? On board one of the galleys was Mary Queen of Scots en route from France to Scotland where she was to find herself confronting John Knox and later, in England, becoming a prisoner of Queen Elizabeth. She had left Calais on 14th August and arrived in Leith on the 19th having encountered fog during the passage.

We know of the fleet's presence in local waters from a letter written by William Strickland who was given eye-witness reports when he arrived in Flamborough on 17th August; the vessels had been anchored close in to Flamborough, South Landing the previous day.

Perhaps the fleet commander had given orders to rendezous there in case vessels became dispersed during the sea crossing. Whatever the reason, William Strickland regretted that circumstances had not brought him to Flamborough one day earlier to enjoy the stirring sight.

There were those who were not prepared to wait for whatever the sea might leave on the shore but would rather set sail to take what they could by force. Pirates were a hazard to shipping on the East Coast through many centuries in spite of attempts to suppress them. In 1565, Queen Elizabeth sent out Commissioners for this purpose and some were ordered to investigate the ports of Scarborough, Filey, Flamborough and Bridlington. Clearly they were not completely successful in their efforts to root out pirates, for in 1578 Filey was listed as having three offenders in piracy; not quite such an infamous record as that resulting from Bridlington's seven and Scarborough's known 22 pirates. What position did these three pirates hold in the community? Did they live with the fishermen and the tillers of the open fields, or did they form a separate group? We shall never know. Much piratical activity centred on Flamborough Head with buccaneering vessels lying in wait off Sewerby and sailing out to surprise vessels rounding Flamborough Head from the north. In 1473 the *Le*

Marye, a Scottish ship, was attacked by a known Flamborough pirate, Robert Constable. A warrant was issued for his arrest but no positive action was taken; possibly because his father, Sir Marmaduke, was lord of the manor.

An encounter at sea which had its humorous side took place in 1744 between a Filey coble and a warship of the Royal Navy; in his diary, George Beswick records how a pistol was fired from the ship to instruct the Filey men to lose way so that the sailors could, by enquiry, establish their position. The fishermen, no doubt misinterpreting the signal, merely waved their caps and cheered enthusiastically. However, the firing of a cannon across their bows soon clarified the warship's intentions and the coble stopped with alacrity.

Filonians must many times have witnessed from Carr Naze, exciting battles at sea. Scarborough, having both castle and harbour, was frequently the setting of quite ferocious fighting. It is recorded that in 1377 a Scottish pirate by the name of Mercer was captured and held in the castle. His son organised a fleet of Scottish, French and Spanish ships and, in a raid, released his father and also captured several vessels from the harbour. This was not the end of the story, as one Alderman Phillpot of London aggrieved by this episode, assembled a large fleet at his own expense, recovered the pirated vessels, recaptured Mercer and took 15 Spanish ships as a bonus. It must sometimes have been difficult to distinguish the goodies from the baddies.

A strange and tragic sea story, with echoes of the *Marie Celeste,* is that of the steamship *Hawkwood.* On 12th January 1913 the vessel was observed off Flamborough Head, apparently crewless, and she was later driven aground under Speeton cliffs. No trace of her captain or seventeen members of the crew was ever found.

Today relatively few vessels passing up and down the coast are observed from Filey. The coastal trade is very much diminished and the shipping lanes for many larger vessels bound for Tees and Tyne are beyond the horizon.

However, in one's imagination may still be seen the Bay filled with hundreds of sailing ships waiting for a storm to abate, or large fleets of laden colliers sailing slowly south. Memory or imagination too recall the wartime convoys of 50 or more ships, some trailing barrage balloons to deter enemy aircraft, and each convoy with its attendant frigates or destroyers on the alert for enemy submarines.

And then one wonders how many dramatic incidents, witnessed, or unwitnessed there have been in that short stretch of sea-way between Scarborough and Flamborough Head which is visible from Carr Naze. No doubt such a catalogue would include 6th century Saxon raiders searching for a landing beach; Viking longships appearing over the horizon; war-time battles and confrontations with pirates and smugglers; horrendous shipwrecks and rescues of outstanding bravery. These few miles of coastline have seen all of these and so much more.

Smuggling

Smuggling has been a major activity around the coasts of Britain as long as Sovereigns and Governments have raised revenue by imposing duties on goods being carried both in and out of the country. The Yorkshire coast, from Humber to Tees, has been witness to the movement of considerable quantities of smuggled goods and to many incidents both dramatic and humorous and also, on occasion, tragic.

By its nature, smuggling was (and is) an activity which endeavours not to draw attention to itself, nor is it one for which those primarily involved keep meticulous records for open inspection. It is therefore certain that we know about only a small fraction of all that took place as men and women sought to bring into (and sometimes take out of) the country a wide variety of goods without the knowledge of the revenue men.

The creeks and inlets of the River Humber were much used, though negotiating sand and mud banks under sail or oar and in the dark must have been both difficult and dangerous. The sands along the Holderness coast had much to recommend them for such purposes as they were relatively easy of access from both sea and land and long stretches were distant from any habitation. The rocks and steep cliffs from Sewerby to Reighton presented obvious dangers in daylight and much more in darkness, as did much of the coast north of Filey, though no doubt men familiar with these parts would not be deterred. Filey Bay itself would be an area that would be seen to have several natural advantages.

In fact, in the early 1800s, General Howard Vyse, who commanded the Militia Regiments engaged in preventative duties on much of the East Coast, identified Filey Bay as one of the areas where there would be an agent who would organise the landing, transport and distribution of contraband goods.

One of the earliest known examples of local smuggling took place in 1298. Edward I, in common with later sovereigns, saw the wool export trade as a convenient source of revenue which could be acquired by means of customs duties and sometimes even expropriation. This no doubt would be the reason why Peter de Blake attempted to ship out 70 sacks of wool secretly through the 'port of Filey'. However, unfortunately for Peter he was not apparently sufficiently skilled in the smuggler's art and he was caught and charged. Some 20 years earlier, seven men, including the Prior of Bridlington, were alleged to have taken 164 sacks of wool to the port of Filey without informing the customs.

In 1367 a vessel carrying coal went aground on Filey Brigg. No doubt it would not be long before the local folk went to see what fortune had brought their way. Hidden under the coal they found to their surprise, and presumably pleasure, a quantity of wool; another illegal export which didn't reach its intended destination.

Although smuggling certainly continued through successive centuries it was from the late 18th and into the 19th century that it became almost a major coastal industry. It was then said that in the fishing villages of Robin Hood's Bay, Staithes, Marske and Runswick Bay, almost the entire population would be involved. This description was never applied to Filey, but perhaps this was not so much because Filonians were of stronger moral fibre than villagers to the north, but rather that Filey Bay was more easily observed and reached by local revenue men and therefore was not so frequently used. However, tradition has it that contraband from the continent came into the country via Filey Bay. Butcher Haven, near Hunmanby Gap, was supposedly one favoured route by which smuggled goods were taken inland under the cover of darkness.

Regrettably many of the revenue records for that part of the coast between Scarborough and Bridlington have been destroyed and therefore no doubt there have been exciting events about which we shall now never know.

Revenue officers had the powers of search; so not only was there danger of discovery as goods were being brought ashore, but also when they had been hidden close to the coast prior to later shipment inland. Recipients of contraband in coastal villages and towns would also have to take more care to avoid detection than customers further inland as the coastal regions were the main field of operation for preventative men. There would no doubt be occasions when goods would be carried surreptitiously along Queen Street during the hours of night. The Ship Inn (now T'Oard Ship — a private house) had as part of its construction a beam, solid in appearance but hollow in reality. Another dwelling became known as the Old Smugglers' Cottage, though why it was so named is uncertain. Now demolished, it was situated just to the south of the most easterly house in Queen Street. Another house with smuggling links was 45 Church Street, which enjoyed a hidden access to the house next door through a sliding panel.

In the 18th and 19th centuries, the estimated loss of revenue to the Crown was so great that soldiers were used to assist the Customs men. The coast in the vicinity of Filey saw much of Scottish troopers of the 2nd Dragoons. They were often stationed in twos and threes in coastal villages and it is doubtful that they were very effective against wiley local men.

Encounters between revenue officers and smugglers took place both on sea and on land. One of the fiercest battles in the annals of contraband running took place off Filey in 1777. The combatants were initially, on the one hand George Fagg in command of the *Kent*, a schooner armed with sixteen 4 pounder guns, and on the other Captains Gillie of the revenue cutters *Prince of Wales* and Ogilvie of the *Royal George*. On July 11th the vessels were close enough for Ogilvie to challenge Fagg; his reply was "Fire away and be damned to you!" The three vessels exchanged shots with some damage to the *Prince of Wales;* the battle being watched with interest by several Filey coble fishermen. It appeared the more heavily armed *Kent* would escape when the frigate HMS. *Pelican* came slowly into view (there was little wind) and the fighting intensified, growing yet more fierce with the arrival of *H.M S. Arethusa*. The long engagement finally ended with several smugglers dead and the schooner taken to Hull as a prize and a considerable amount of spirits and tea impounded.

As late as 1884 it was reported that heavy smuggling was taking place on the Yorkshire coast and Flamborough fishermen were bringing in tobacco, cigars and eau de cologne; it appears that no Filey men were engaged in these illegal imports.

Smuggling, we know, goes on today, though sadly it is often of more dangerous substances than the coffee, silk and brandy of earlier days. No longer is it an activity either, in which almost whole village communities might engage themselves. What was frequently regarded as a game is now an activity more deadly in nature.

Harbour Schemes

There have been many proposed schemes for building a harbour at Filey, and for these proposals there have been three basic reasons.

The earliest reason was as a harbour of refuge for sailing ships caught by adverse weather conditions; another reason was for the import and export of general cargo, and thirdly to facilitate the landing of fish and the maintenance of fishing vessels.

Anyone familiar with the Yorkshire Coast will appreciate that it was a most dangerous one for sailing ships, particularly when there were adverse wind and weather conditions. From Medieval times until the late 19th century the East Coast was a well-used shipping lane for vessels under sail. The coal trade between the Tyne and the Thames employed a considerable number of colliers and the general state of the main roads meant that the sea was often the preferred route by which travellers would journey between Scotland and England. Frequently, other vessels would be occupied in the Baltic Trade, or sailing to and from North Sea, European and distant ports. On the 18th May 1744, George Beswick of Gristhorpe recorded in his diary, after walking up to Gristhorpe Cliff, "There was a great fleet of loaden ships computed to upwards of two hundred sail of Colleris (colliers) steering Southward, and a much less number sailing to the North". What a stirring sight that must have been. On occasions when sea conditions were such that Flamborough Head was too difficult to negotiate, it was possible to see, in the 19th century, literally hundreds of sailing ships riding out the storm in Filey Bay. Because of the exposed nature of the Yorkshire coast and the few natural havens for shipping it was long thought that Filey Bay had much to recommend it as a Harbour of Refuge.

Perhaps the earliest positive action was that taken in December 1637 by Lady Ouchterlony and Thomas Talbot, (Lady Ouchterlony was the widow of Sir James, a Gentleman of the Privy Chamber of King James I who had taken a close interest in the safety of coastal shipping). They prepared a plan for a harbour of refuge in Filey Bay. However, Hull Trinity House reported to London Trinity House that this would be 'unusefull and needless'.

Some years later, in December 1661, Sir John and Lady Bucke and others resident in Filey, requested Hull Trinity House to send representatives to report on the suitability of Filey Bay for such a harbour. Leonard Cawood and Andrew Raikes reported favourably on such a project. However, nothing was done.

Although Capt. W. Hewitt, R.N., in 1836, gave evidence before a Select Committee in support of a Harbour of Refuge, no action was taken.

In 1858, John Coode prepared a report on a 'Proposed Harbour of Refuge'. He began his report by pointing out that on 8th December 1857, 240 vessels were anchored in the south part of the Bay and that some years previous 750 vessels had been counted at one time in the Bay. For such an occasion the phrase 'a forest of masts' must surely have been entirely appropriate. Mr. Coode's plan was for breakwaters enclosing much of the Bay at an estimated cost of £860,000 — a considerable sum. Again, no further action was taken.

The next development was in 1864 when the Filey Fishing Harbour Company obtained permission to construct a quay and breakwater, but as no further steps were taken, permission expired five years later.

The most ambitious commercial scheme was proposed in 1869. This involved a breakwater from the Brigg extending south east along the Spittals up to a length of about 850 feet and another extending straight into the Bay from Church Ravine — a distance of about 3300 feet. Associated with the scheme were quays, sheds, a dry dock, railway connections through Church Ravine, and a new estate on the cliffs. Perhaps fortunately, this scheme had no more success than its predecessors.

The next scheme was planned on similar lines, but was much less ambitious. It was prepared by the Filey Fishery Harbour and Pier Co. Ltd. The company's first ordinary meeting took place on 18th May 1878 with Lord Claud Hamilton as Chairman, just after he had addressed 200 fishermen members of the Order of Oddfellows from the Crescent Hotel balcony. The capital cost was estimated to be of the order of £100,000. In 1880 the Filey Harbour Act was passed, but again no material progress was made and in November 1883 the company was wound up. No further serious attempts to construct a harbour have been made.

One reason advanced for building a large commercial harbour here was that Filey was several miles closer than Hull to the Baltic. If such a project had actually been completed there is no doubt that Filey, both as a community and as a resort, would have been vastly changed.

CHAPTER EIGHT

Recent Developments

The final years of the 20th Century and the short succeeding period to the present day have seen in Filey, as in so many other communities, some considerable changes. The Brigg, the Bay, and the beach, together with the town's promenade and spacious parks and gardens, remain the features which continue to attract visitors in significant numbers throughout a gradually extending Season. The considerable reduction in the number of boarding-houses and hotels in Filey since the early post-war years, however, means that fewer holiday-makers seen here now actually stay in the town but this reduction is more than balanced by those staying at holiday venues outside the town.

It is now 180 years since Filey began to develop from a fishing village into a highly regarded holiday resort and the process of change has continued during that period but, of course, at very varying rates. If the built environment is considered, the recent three decades have seen some of the most rapid rates of change. During those years Filey's commercial heart has remained essentially the same although Chapel Court, a development of apartments, replaced a motor business in the town centre. Another major change was the total demolition of Filey's gas-works close to the Railway Station; it supplied Filey with town gas for more than a century until the introduction of natural gas. The contaminated site has also now been cleared and there are approved plans for a supermarket and car-park but, as yet, the site remains undeveloped.

Other small residential properties have been built within the town but most new building has taken place as the town has extended its boundaries on to previously open land within the area designated as being available for housing. The two main new residential developments close to the Dams nature reserve and to Seadale are significantly different from the estates which preceded them (Wharfedale and Parish Fields) in having within them a much wider variety of homes. The rapidity with which these properties were sold confirmed that, in addition to those who retire here, there are those for whom Filey is seen to be a good place in which to live while working elsewhere.

The increase in Filey's built area has, however, contributed to the heightened risk of flooding and this led, in 2007, to the spirited opposition by local groups and by Town and Borough Councils to a proposal to build a totally new estate of 300 houses between Muston Road and Seadale. However, to the consternation of many, the plan was accepted by the Department of the

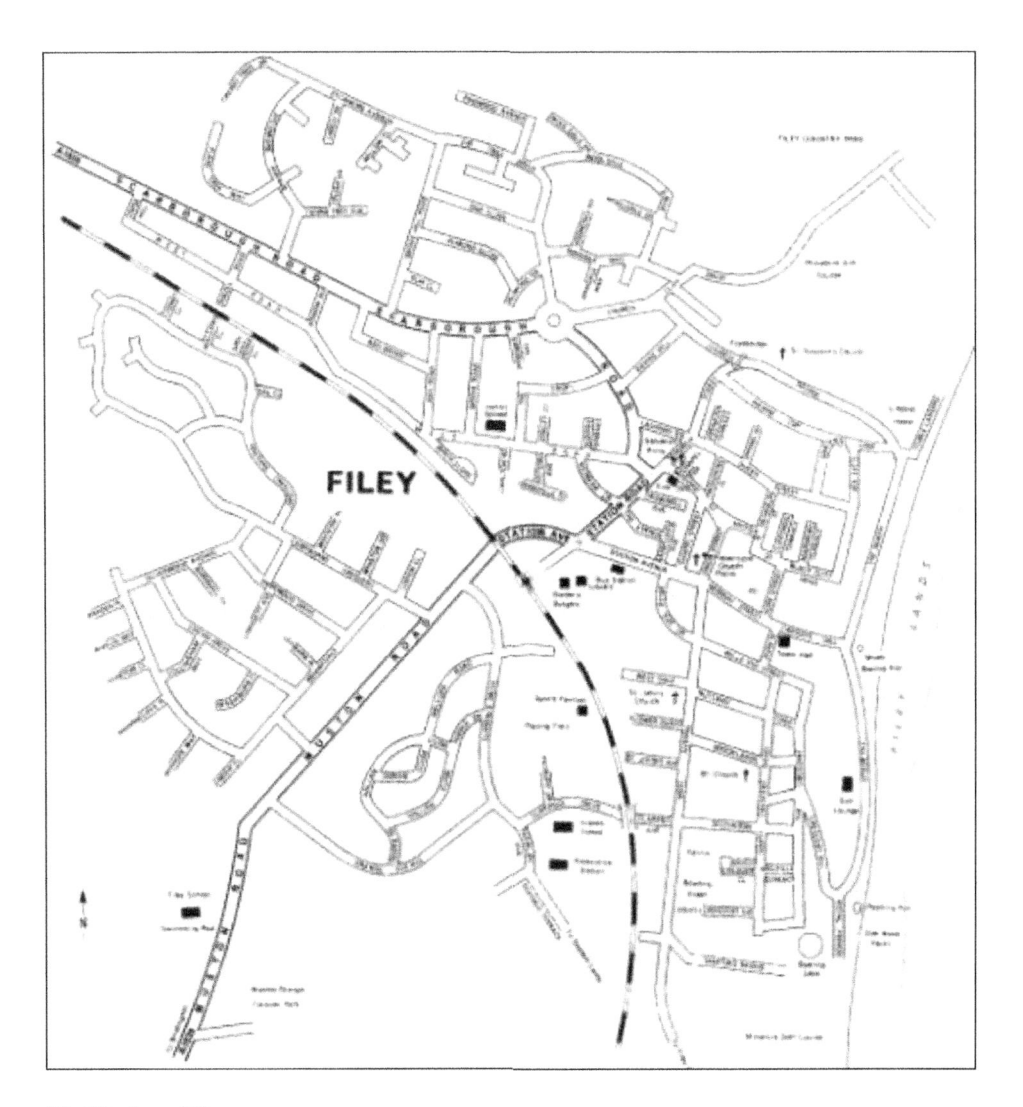

59. Modern Filey.

Environment and although several important conditions were attached to the acceptance, townspeople were not reassured.

The relatively recent anxiety about flooding here is understandable; when such events occurred elsewhere, perhaps in Malton or York, Filonians would confidently predict that "Filey will never flood!" However, in August 2002, as a result of a lengthy period of torrential rain, several parts of the town were subject to serious flooding. In the succeeding months and years efforts were made to identify and to remedy the causes; it was a cause for major concern therefore in July 2007 when many of those who suffered in 2002 found themselves, once again, having to leave their homes and move into temporary accommodation which, for some, consisted of caravans positioned on their drives. Efforts continue at several levels of responsibility in attempts to ensure that such distressing and expensive events do not occur again.

One major development which took place in 2001 and was widely welcomed was the significant improvement to the promenade and Foreshore carried out by Yorkshire Water and Scarborough Borough Council. The impetus for this work was the perceived need to upgrade the treatment of waste water and large underground tanks were installed to avoid, in times of heavy rain, surface water being discharged on to the beach. Associated with this work was the building of a new sewage treatment plant one mile inland near Muston railway crossing. This new system ensures that the water discharged from the farthest point of the Brigg is sufficiently clean for the sea-water in Filey Bay to be judged to be of an acceptably high standard.

In 1998, Filey's largest new building was built, overlooking the promenade; erected on what had been, originally, the grounds of a single family home, Deepdene is a development of fifty apartments which, after some initial uncertainty, is now regarded by many as being perhaps the finest development of its kind on the Yorkshire Coast.

Butlin's Holiday Camp was a major part of Filey's post-war history for 39 years and its closure in the Autumn of 1983 was an economic blow from which it has taken the community a long time to recover. After 25 and more years many visitors to Filey continue to recall with real pleasure holidays at the Camp with its wide range of facilities and relaxed atmosphere.

Following its closure there followed a period of uncertainty regarding its future until, in 1986 the site was purchased and re-established as a holiday venue under the name of Amtree Park with Ernie Wise performing the opening ceremony. However, the whole enterprise was seriously under-funded, and came to an end after only six weeks during which period many who had taken concessions there lost much of their financial investment.

There then followed several years of gradual decline which caused much concern to those who observed it, and particularly to those who had had associations with Butlin's during its peak years as the World's largest holiday camp. It was also seen as a very valuable asset to Filey which was slowly disintegrating. In the course of these years proposals were made about the future use of the site but local people found it difficult to take these seriously when even the ownership of the land was at times under query. Finally, in 2005, an application was approved for what is destined to become, effectively, a new town with the name 'The Bay'. The sheer scale of the new development with its several hundred residential properties and associated facilities took residents here greatly by surprise. At the present time (2008), building is taking place there rapidly and, of course, is being followed with interest by many as the site enters a new phase in its 70 years history.

In 1905 the Sisters of Charity of Our Lady of Evron (in Normandy) opened the Convent of the Sacred Heart and for 64 years it was a highly regarded boarding and day school for girls. On its closure the building was purchased by Filey Urban District Council and it became Filey's Town Hall; in

60. Filey Beach in 2008.

1974, on local government reorganisation, it became the responsibility of Scarborough Borough Council, and the newly-formed Filey Town Council remained in the building as tenants.

In 1993 the building in Queen Street which Filey Urban District Council built as Council Offices in 1898 but which the Council had had to vacate at the commencement of World War Two, was purchased by the Town Council and, after an interval of 54 years the Council was able to return. This afforded the opportunity for the assembling of a collection of files, documents, minute books, photographs and newspapers which is now known as the Crimlisk-Fisher Archive. John Crimlisk was a dedicated local historian and Walter Fisher had taken, professionally, many photographs of Victorian Filey. Following the appointment of an Honorary Archivist the collection has developed into one of the finest archives established by a Parish or Town Council in Britain and, for reference purposes, is open to the public.

Two other major buildings which have been restored in recent years are the former Grand Cinema and Ebenezer Methodist Church, both situated in Union Street. The Grand has become The Buccaneer, a bar, entertainment centre and restaurant and Ebenezer, which for some years had been a builder's store and workshop has been, on the initiative of three young local men, transformed into an imaginative development of apartments. The restoration of the imposing façade was especially gratifying to those who had had close links with the former Church.

The receipt of a significant grant from European funding enabled the Borough Council to convert the much under-used Town Hall into a widely appreciated community facility. Because of the building's early history, the name it was given was the Evron Centre. Available there now are rooms for hire, offices for small businesses, an improved Concert Hall and a much extended Tourist Information Centre.

As described in Chapter Seven, fishing has been important to Filey for perhaps more than a thousand years; today it is still a significant part of Filey's economy but it has diminished in recent years to a point where there are serious concerns about its future. At present, about five cobles are engaged in commercial fishing, primarily for shell-fish and a vital factor in their operation is the availability of a tractor for launching and recovering the boats. If the number of cobles should be further reduced, maintaining a tractor on the Coble Landing would become more difficult.

From several points of view, professional fishing here is still so important that it is profoundly to be hoped that it will continue well into the future as a viable enterprise.

In the same way as do members of almost any other community, residents of Filey have concerns about its future particularly when significant changes are taking place. Although efforts in recent years to extend Filey's industrial base met with only limited success we know that pressures from national and regional government to build more houses are being experienced across the country. However, locally, many residents of and visitors to Filey believe that the town has reached both its optimum size and population and that, fortunately, it has retained those qualities of a small town which are still much valued.

It is to be hoped that Filey's future role will continue to be that of a community of which it is good to be a member and also that of a resort in which to spend time on holiday is a fully rewarding experience.

APPENDIX A

Population Changes

1672 ………..77 Households
1743…………..c. 120 families
1763……...……c. 105 families

1801 : 505	1871 : 2267	1941 : -
1811 : 579	1881 : 2337	1951 : 4765
1821 : 773	1891 : 2481	1961 : 4703
1831 : 802	1901 : 3003	1971 : 5336
1841 : 1231	1911 : 3228	1981 : 5460
1851 : 1511	1921 : 4549	1991 : 6619
	(includes visitors)	2001 : 6468
1861 : 1881	1931 : 3733	2006 : 6880 (Estimated)

APPENDIX B

Some versions of the name of Filey:

Fucelac	...	1086
Fivelei	...	1096
Fyvele	...	12th Century
Phyvelay	...	1139
Fiflea	...	1196
Fyeley	...	1565
Fyley	...	1650
Philaw		
Filo		
Ffyley		

SOURCES OF INFORMATION

The following is a list of information sources; most are, of course, now out of print, but several are available through the North Yorkshire County Council Library Service.

Of particular value is the Victoria County History section on Filey; it contains a wealth of detail and a comprehensive list of references.

1. Filey Parish Registers.
2. The History & Antiquities of Filey In The County Of York.
   John Cole. Printed & Published by J. Cole. 1828.
3. Filey Census Returns.
4. Observations On Filey as a Watering Place.
   E.W. Pritchard, M.D., M.R.C.S.
   George L. Beeforth, 3 St. Nicholas Street, Scarborough. 1853
5. A Historical Account of the Herring Fishery of the North-East Coast of England.
   William S. Cortis. 1858
6. An Historical and Descriptive Guide to Filey.
   William S. Cortis, M.D. 1860.
7. Minutes of Evidence of the Sea Fisheries Commission. Witnesses at Filey, 1st October 1863.
   Commission Members: James Caird, M.P., and Professor T.H. Huxley. Questions 5673 to 6412.
8. Rambles About Filey.
   George Shaw.
   Published by Hamilton, Adams & Co., Paternoster Row, London. 1867.
9. Our Filey Fishermen
   Rev. George Shaw.
   Published by Hamilton, Adams & Co. 1867
10. Filey Post. 1871 - 1916.
11. Filey And Its Church. A.N. Cooper. 1889.
12. Folk-Lore of East Yorkshire.
    John Nicholson.
    (First Published 1890). E.P. Publishing Ltd. 1973.
13. Filey Sea-Wall.
    E. Martin and A.N. Cooper. 1894.
14. Theakston's Illustrated Guide to Filey. A.N. Cooper. c. 1902.
15. A Guide To Old Filey. W.H. Oxley. 1912.
16. York and District Trades Directory. 1912-13.
17. Scarborough, Filey, Scalby & District Directory. 1915. W.H. Smith & Son, 31A St. Nicholas Street, Scarborough.
18. Filey News. 1931-1955.

180

19. Sail and Oar, a Hundred Pictures. Ernest Dade.
J.M. Dent & Sons Ltd., London. 1933.
20. Oh! Little Filey.
M. Andrews.
R. Milward & Sons Ltd., Lenton, Nottingham. 1946.
21. The Story of Filey.
M. Andrews.
(First Published 1946).
M.J. Milward, 29 Sandalwood Road, Loughborough.
5th Edition.
22. Hunmanby, East Yorkshire, a Story of Ten Centuries.
Lucy M. Owston.
Printed for Author by G.A. Pinder & Son, Scarborough. 1948.
23. The Heart of Filey.
M. Andrews.
W.H. Lead Ltd., Silver Street, Leicester. 1949.
24. Newspaper Articles.
George Waller.
25. The Beginnings of the East Yorkshire Railways.
K.A. MacMahon.
East Yorkshire Local History Society 1953.
26. Filey Holiday Guides.
27. The Agricultural Revolution in The East Riding.
Olga Wilkinson.
East Yorkshire Local History Society. 1955.
28. Charlotte Bronte on the East Yorkshire Coast.
F.R. Pearson.
East Yorkshire Local History Society. 1957.
29. Filey Advertiser. 1957-1963.
30. Primary Education in East Yorkshire. 1560-1902.
J. Lawson.
East Yorkshire Local History Society. 1959.
31. The Viking Century in East Yorkshire.
A.L. Binns.
East Yorkshire Local History Society.1963.
32. Local History Articles. John Crimlisk.
33. Militia, Yeomanry and Voluntary Forces of the East Riding. 1689-1908.
R.W.S. Norfolk.
East Yorkshire Local History Society. 1965.
34. Pom-Poms and Ruffles.
G.J. Mellor.
Dalesman Publishing Co. Ltd. 1966.
35. Domesday Book and the East Riding.
F.W. Brooks.
East Yorkshire Local History Society. 1966.
36. East Yorkshire in the Sagas.
A.L. Binns.
East Yorkshire Local History Society. 1966,
37. A History of Flamborough.
Frank Brearley.
Ridings Publishing Co., Driffield. 1971.
38. Buildings of England. Yorkshire: York and the East Riding.
Nikolaus Pevsner.
Penguin Books. 1972.

39. The Victoria History of the County of York: East Riding, Volume II.
Published for the University of London Institute of Historical Research by Oxford University Press, London. 1974.

40. Shipwrecks of the Yorkshire Coast. Arthur Godfrey and Peter J. Lassey. Dalesman Books. 1974.

41. Yorkshire Fishing Fleets. Arthur Godfrey.
Dalesman Books. 1974.

42. Railways in Yorkshire. 2: The East Riding.
K. Hoole.
Dalesman Books. 1976.

43. Excavations at Filey. 1976. Peter G. Farmer.
Published by PG. & N.C. Farmer for Filey Local History Society,
The Museum, 8-10 Queen Street, Filey.

44. Smuggling on the Yorkshire Coast. Jack Dykes.
Dalesman Books. 1978.

45. Remember Scarborough 1914! David Mould. Hendon Publishing Co. Ltd., Nelson, Lancashire. 1978.

46. Geology of the Yorkshire Coast. Stephen Young.
Dalesman Books. 1978.

47. The English Coble. H.O. Hill. National Maritime Museum. 1978.

48. Yorkshire Place-Names. William Thurlow.
Dalesman Books. 1979.

49. Golf-Lima-Foxtrot-Echo. A Story of the Filey Lifeboat. Jeff Morris.

50. A History of Gristhorpe. Diana Beswick. c.1980.

51. Yorkshire's Early Flying Days, a Pictorial History. Ronald Nelson Redman. Dalesman Books. 1981.

52. The Railways of East Yorkshire. C.T. Goode.
The Oakwood Press, 1981.

53. Local History Articles. James Brown.

54. Filey Bay. J.C. Ellis.

55. Light Up The World. The Story of Leonard Dale and Dale Electric. 1935-1985.
Hugh Barty-King.
Quiller Press, London. 1985.

56. Filey: A Yorkshire Fishing Town. Irene Allen and Andrew Todd. Published by Authors. 1985.

57. The Postal History of Bridlington, Filey and Hunmanby.
Ronald Ward and William A. Sedgewick.
Yorkshire Postal History Society. Publication No.18. June 1985.

58. A Village At War. (Hunmanby During World War II).

59. A History of the Yorkshire Coast Fishing Industry 1780-1914.
Robb Robinson.
Hull University Press. 1987

60. Archive Material
Kenneth Clegg.

182

INDEX

Ackroyd, R M 127
Amtree Park 174
Anglo-Saxons 9
Ardens 62
Armada 19
Artillery Volunteers **37**, 38
Aukland, Lord 60

bathing machines 41
Bay Court Development 90
Bentley, Henry 82
Beswick, George 170
Bethesda Chapel 103
Blackburn Aircraft Company 57
Blackburn, Robert 57
Blake, Peter de 168
Board of Health 31
Boer War 41
Brig Cinema 90
Bronte, Charlotte 133
Bucke family 18
Bucke, Sir John 22, 171
Butlin, William 139
Butlins Camp 76, 136, **137, 138**

Caine, Andie 136
Carr Naze 2
Celestine III, Pope 142
Chambers, P C 42
Charles I, King 22, 145
Church Cliff Drive 74
cinemas 76
Civil War 21
Clarence House 91, 113
Clarke, John 20

Cliff House 83
coal 165
Coastguard Station 89
Cockrell, William 20
Conservative Party 117
Constable family 18
Coode, John 171
Cooper, Rev A N 94, 100
Council School 112
Country Park 80
coxswains 161
Crescent 87, 122
Crescent Gardens 125
Crescent Hotel **45**
Crimlisk, John 176

Dale Electric 120
Daniel, J H 112
Deepdene 174
Delius, Frederick 132
Domesday Book 12
Drake, Charlie 140

Ebenezer Chapel 104, **105**, 176
Edge, Charles 29
Edith Cavell 157
education 110
elections 116
Elizabeth I, Queen 18, 166
Emera 15
enclosure 26
Evron Centre 113, 176

Farrar, Dean 129
Filey Advertiser 114

Filey Gas Company 31
Filey Harbour Act 171
Filey Museum 81
Filey News 136
Filey Post 113, 133
Filey Road 62
Filey Spa 124
Filey Town Council 81
Filey Urban District Council 33, 73
Filey Waterworks Company 31
fishing 142
flooding 172
Foord, Thomas 31, 121
Foreshore Road 80
Friendly Societies 35
Furley, Reynold 20

Gage, Henry 42
Gant, Gilbert de 18
Gant, Walter de 14
Gibson, Walter 120
Goff, Clarence 116
Grand Cinema 89
Grand Theatre 51

Hamilton, Lord Claud 171
harbour schemes 170
Hawkwood 167
Henry VIII, King 17
herring fishing 150
Hinderwell, Thomas 160
Hindle, Ben 72
Hoggart, Richard 76
Hollon, R W 160
hotels 123
House, John 56
Hucks, B C 57
Hudson, George 109
Hull 157
Huntress, Elizabeth 28

Infants' School 110

Integrity 145
Iron Church 101

James I, King 21
Jenkinson family 155
Jenkinson, John W 118
Jenkinson, Matthew 33
John Street 38, 113
Jones, John Paul 24
Junior School 112

Kendall, Rev G 153
Kendals 119
Kirk, H R 58

Labour Party 117
Laundry 91
Le Marye 167
Legard, Sir Charles 41
Leopold II, King 133
Liberal Party 117
Lifeboat Day 162
Lifeboat Service 160
Lutton, William 16

market 14
Marr, Thomas **64**
Martin 166
Martin, Edward 33, 116
Methodists 101
Mitford Street 76
Morley, John 119
Murray Street 48, 68
Muston Rd 17

Nansen Café 54
Newlands 89
Northcliffe 91

occupations 93
Old Filey 92
Osbaldeston family 19, 28

Osborne House 62
Overy, Charles 119
Overy, Richard 155
Oxtoby, John 102

Page, John 165
Pelican HMS 162, 169
pierrots 51, 135
pilots 57
poll tax 15
population 20, 23, 29, 31
Primrose Valley 68, 95
Princess Royal 134
Pritchard, Dr E 118

Quakers 27, 107
Queen Street 2, 16, 41, 82, **84,** 89, 94, 169

R N L I 160
railway 107
Ranfurly, Earl of 131
Ravine Hall 82
Reekie, Lister 114, **115,** 136
Reighton Gap 3
Rickman, Katherine 20
Roman Jetty 6
Rowe, Robert 28
Royal Crecent Hotel 58, 87
Royal Filey Pierrots 136
Rutland Terrace 87

Salt, Titus 132
Salvation Army 107
sea defence 46
sea wall 44
Secondary School 112

Shakesby, Albert 118
Signal Station 7
smuggling 168
Smyth, Robert 20
Southdene Pavilion 68
Spa Saloon 89
St Bartholomew's Chapel 16
St John's Church 101
St Mary's 106
St Oswald's Church **10,** 14, 96, **97, 99**
stagecoaches 121
Staintondale Hunt 38
Stork, Robert 35
storm of 1869 153

Talbot, Thomas 170
The Bay 174
Town Hall 87
Tranmer, J W F, 56
Trinity Chapel 104
Trinity Methodist Church 63

Unett, John Wilkes 31, 83, 127
Union Street 89

Victoria Hall 51
Vikings 11
visitor lists 128
Vyse, General Howard 168

West Avenue 73
William I, King 12
William II, King 13
Williams, Rev E 98

yards 93

Other Yorkshire History books from the Blackthorn Press are available as paperbacks or ebooks.

Roman Yorkshire, Anglian York, Viking Age Yorkshire, Early Tudor Yorkshire, Yorkshire in the Reign of Elizabeth I, History of Driffield, History of Northallerton, History of Ryedale, History of Selby, History of Scarborough, Scarborough's Heroes, Rogues and Eccentrics, History of Richmond, History of Hornsea, History of York, History of Whitby, History of Beverley, History of Pickering, History of Seamer, History of Thornton-le-Dale, Villages of East Yorkshire, The Story of York, The Story of Hull, The Story of Bradford, The Story of Pickering, Marston Moor, Adwalton Moor, Yorkshire in the Civil Wars, Whitby Pickering and Scarborough Railway, Sir Hugh Cholmley, The Rowntree Family of York, J R Mortimer, The Yorkshire Mary Rose, Religion in Yorkshire, Francis Nicholson, Victorian Ships, A Fine Eye for Colour.

English Literature from the Blackthorn Press includes:

D H Lawrence: Complete Short Stories, Complete Travel Writing, Complete Plays, Complete Essays, Complete Novellas and all the novels. Wilfred Owen Complete Poems, William Wordsworth Selected Poems, Brontë Sisters Selected Poems, Truth is Not Sober, Trollope Complete Short Stories and many other titles available as paperback or ebook.

All these and other titles are available from our website www.blackthornpress.com or from the Amazon website.